Colours of the Mind

A DOG TRAINING GUIDE

your dog would choose

LoveK9: *Colours of the Mind*

ISBN: 978-0-9956199-2-0

Published by Brian Stanton

Copy Edited by Brian Stanton

Cover Design by Charles Leveroni

Printed and bound by IngramSpark

Vector images used under license from Shutterstock.com

Acknowledgements

To my wonderful mother, brother, sister-in-law and other family members in Ireland … and many friends and family in England who have all been looking forward to this book being published—thank you all for your patience and support.

Clare McDermott, Richard Clayton, Helen Foord, Caroline Brockdorff, Sue Chalcraft, Noemi Kormos, Jan Hunter, Margaret Moore and Caroline Roberts have all helped proofread this text and offered very valuable feedback … thank you so much for your time, feedback and encouragement. It's taken a while but we got there in the end!

To those who volunteered—themselves and their dogs—to demonstrate training techniques in front of the camera: Jean Dench, Vicky Browning, Teresa Fry, John McGrory, Margaret Moore, Tiddy De Rokeby, Helen Foord, Ryan and Millie Crosby-Foord, Tom and Jo Waring, Shirley Williams—thank you (and your fabulous dogs) for being so positive and helpful throughout.

Thanks must go to Richard Clayton for taking many of the images that feature here and for recording some of the LoveK9 video clips that are available online. Many thanks to Charles Leveroni for doing an excellent job designing the book cover.

Helen Foord, Jean Dench, Vicky Browning, Noemi Kormos, Caroline Brockdorff (with 'Dr Chigs'), Tiddy De Rokeby, Andy & Sue Smith, Margaret Moore, Jan Ní Bhraonáin and Sue Chalcraft have always been so supportive re: LoveK9 and have helped *so many* dogs over the years in different ways. Your ongoing commitment to education and animal welfare is admirable and really appreciated.

Dave and Tel German—thank you for always being so kind and generous ... letting us use your land to safely exercise, train and help dogs in different ways.

To the very many owners and dogs I've met over the years ... thank you. All of our LoveK9 trainers are very grateful—we have learnt so much from all of you.

Finally, thank *you* so much for purchasing this book. I hope you enjoy reading it.

CONTENTS

Preface 1

COMMUNICATION

1 The Power of Vibe 7
2 Colours of the Mind 17
3 Understanding Praise 21
4 Guidance and Correction 31
5 The Value of Exercise 45

ESSENTIAL COMMANDS

6 Your Approach to Training 55
7 Sit—*Put your bottom on the floor* 61
8 Wait—*Relax with me* 67
9 Stay—*Don't move out of position* 73
10 Come—*Come back to me* 81
11 Nicely or Gently—*Be gentle with your mouth* 95
12 Close or Heel—*Walk nicely beside me* 101

MANNERS

13 Respect 117
14 Behaviour at Home 121
15 Dog Yoga 127
16 Using Food Wisely 131
17 Laps and Furniture 147
18 Grooming 153

ENJOYING YOUR DOG

19	Play and train	161
20	Fetch, Frisbee and Tug	165
21	Roller Blading, Cycling, Running and Swimming	175
22	Obedience Training	181
23	Agility, Flyball and Ringcraft	187
24	Gundog Training	195
25	Tracking and SAR	199
26	Lure Coursing	201
27	Therapy Dogs	205

VALUABLE COMMANDS

28	Watch—*Look at me and focus on me*	213
29	Down—*Put your tummy on the floor*	217
30	Leave—*Do not move towards*	225
31	This Way—*Follow my direction*	231
32	Stand—*Stand still*	235

PROBLEMS and SOLUTIONS

33	Jumping Up or Lunging	243
34	Separation Anxiety	253
35	Getting Very Excited in the Car	269
36	Fireworks, Storms and Loud Noises	277

Conclusion 287

Preface

Hopes and aspirations

Having trained dogs for well over thirty years, it was very tricky when writing to get 'all the important stuff' down on paper and figure out how to frame things. Deciding what to include (and what to leave out) alongside how everything should flow was a real challenge. So, early on, I looked for direction by asking myself, "what do I want *you* to get out of this? ... what are my goals for you, the reader?" Setting you on the road to becoming an accomplished dog handler as well as equipping you with the tools and confidence to truly enjoy your dog—and vice versa—are definitely aspirations. Sharing strategies and techniques I use when trying to understand, shape or change behaviour is an important aim too. Also, I want you to really appreciate the impact our varied (human) behaviour has on our dogs and encourage you to hone in on the changes you can make yourself, so you can influence and teach your trainee more easily.

Puppy school

While puppies and 'young dogs' are mentioned throughout this book, specific sections or chapters haven't been devoted exclusively to puppy behaviour. Given that a puppy is a young dog forming, the approach to training outlined here—related to 'dogs' in general—is completely relevant to puppies and young dogs as well. The general advice to follow when teaching any juvenile mind is to use a *very* patient and positive approach, one that fuels learning and accommodates your individual dog's age and nature—with (good) common-sense present in everything you do. Setting clear weekly goals and being very consistent in training, as well as having lots of fun of course, are all key factors when conditioning good behaviour in any dog, young or old.

Turning the page

You might realise while reading that maybe you could have behaved differently towards your own dog at home and wish you could roll back the clock and do things all over again. Fortunately for us, dogs tend not to dwell on previous events for very long and most easily adapt and react to new routines and changes in our behaviour very quickly, if these are presented correctly. So, if you really focus on making positive changes in your own behaviour around your dog, it stands to reason that he'll change for the better too.

Having thought about this, you might need to turn the page on the past in your own mind. Congratulate yourself for what you've done well and forgive yourself and your dog for any previous misunderstandings. Start afresh. Once your trainee sees that a new system is in place, he'll love learning and the clarity this new approach provides—at last someone is taking the time to teach him what to do and how to behave. Brilliant.

Dominance and Submission

Terms like 'Dominance' and 'Submission' are often *very* controversial and are often misused and misinterpreted—only causing confusion and great distraction. As a result, I avoid referring to them altogether when discussing any dog in training and use the term 'teacher' to refer to the trainer—you—and 'trainee' when referring to your dog, as these terms accurately reflect our balanced, fair and very positive approach to educating and schooling. By keeping things simple, we can get a straightforward grasp of the helpful training ideas being shared here and avoid getting too distracted and bogged down by terminology.

Gender

As you've already seen in this section, 'him' is used instead of 'him or her' when referring to a dog, for no other reason than it became very awkward when writing (and reading) to use both genders every time. For simplicity, the masculine case is used whenever this kind of thing crops up.

Being thorough

As an owner or prospective owner of a puppy or older dog, it's definitely a wise move on your part to learn how to behave around him and figure out how to communicate effectively with him. Really taking the time to get inside your dog's head and understand his perspective of the world will benefit every aspect of your life with your dog and, of course, his life with you.

Please try to read each section in the order presented, as there are some references in later sections to earlier material. If your approach to learning about 'how things look from your dog's perspective' is focused and determined, you'll be able to understand and modify behaviour as well as bond with your dog at a deeper level very quickly. So, even if you aren't too interested in reading about 'Separation Anxiety,' for example, try not to skip it—what you learn in this section is likely to improve your ability to understand where your dog is coming from in other areas of his life.

Whatever age or breed of dog you have at home, I really hope you learn a lot from reading this insight into your dog's perspective—teach him how to behave well and enjoy amazing times together.

Brian

COMMUNICATION

Chapter 1

The Power of Vibe

We all know that feeling we get when meeting someone for the first time and the impact this has on our perception of them, instantly influencing whether we want to spend time with them, listen and learn from them—or not. This feeling, vibe or energy that's exchanged is of course very important when people interact with one another and is a key factor when dogs communicate with fellow canines … and with people—gauging and sensing our vibrations, our very being, well before any physical contact is made.

What vibe are we giving?

It's very important that we become more aware of the vibe we share with our dogs and consider how we can improve this at times. Becoming self-aware is crucial to improving our individual vibe.

Ask yourself, 'How do I appear from my dog's point of view?' When you pick up your lead to begin a walk and your dog jumps around like he's possessed … how do you react and behave? Does your vibe change when someone comes to the front door and he starts barking? What vibe do you share when he does brilliantly in a training lesson? What vibe do you share when you see an off-lead dog running towards you in the park? What vibe do you share when you feed him? In short, what emotional state are you in? … anxious, confident, trusting, happy, sad, excitable, relaxed or angry … or maybe a combination of these? How does this affect your physical state and the overall reaction/vibe you share with your trainee at different times each day? Think about it. What do you 'feel like' and 'look like' from his perspective? Is it appropriate—the best it could be—or could you improve your vibe sometimes? Maybe you could be a little calmer and more confident in certain situations or are there times when it would be better to share a more animated or excited vibe? … or do you feel you could share your positive 'teacher vibe' more often? Being honest with ourselves and evaluating how we appear from our dog's perspective is a great starting point when exploring how to communicate effectively with any trainee.

Okay, so if it's really important to present ourselves with a *good vibe,* how can we achieve this?

Be a great teacher

Most dogs (and people) listen and respond willingly and attentively to people who present a vibe that is positive, engaging and confident. So, we should try (hard) to remain upbeat, clear and level-headed whenever we're around our trainees, avoiding becoming negative or frustrated as much as we can. Be positive and FUN to be around and do your best to be confident and self-assured. Whenever you interact with your trainee, take a moment to put yourself into this positive, relaxed and confident 'teacher-like' state of mind beforehand. Making any extra effort to present yourself appropriately and give off 'very good vibrations' when spending time with your dog is likely to pay great dividends elsewhere.

Reading your trainee's vibe

Given that your dog is probably very skilled at reading *you* already and is quite familiar with the vibe(s) you share with him at different times in the day, as his teacher, it's important to try to really understand your trainee and appreciate where *he* is coming from in different situations. Knowing your trainee will help your relationship blossom. Try to become adept at reading his vibe each day, building up a clear picture of his likes and dislikes, while making a mental note of times when his vibe alters. Ask yourself ... when is his vibe at its happiest? Is it when a certain food treat or toy is on offer? Maybe game playing in the park with his dog friends 'does it' for your dog? Does your trainee ever share an anxious vibe? ... maybe this happens when he meets some larger breeds in the park? Are there times at home when he gets 'super excited?' Have you ever noticed an aggressive vibe? ... and so on. Observe your friend daily and quietly study his vibe—this will help you anticipate shifts in behaviour and help you interact with him more effectively in the future.

Facial expressions matter

Domestic dogs are known to examine our facial expressions so we should use this knowledge to our advantage when interacting with them. If you're pleased with your trainee, saying a simple 'Good boy' or 'Thank you' or 'Yes' enthusiastically will change your facial expression and your dog will immediately glean that you're pleased with him. If you want to communicate 'Very well done!' then feel free to exaggerate your positive facial expression too just as you say, "Gooood boy!!" If you ever feel you need to show a little disapproval, using a frown alongside a verbal 'No' or 'Ah-Ah' often does the trick.

Even though it might seem like an obvious thing to do, remember to express yourself facially—it will enhance your vibe and the whole communication process will benefit.

Tone of voice and visual cues

We will focus on 'cues' again in later sections, but it's important to note early on that any skilled dog owner/teacher will often use a positive tone of voice (verbal cue) alongside a clear hand-signal (visual cue) when teaching any new behaviour (like 'Come' or 'Stay' for example), making it really easy for their trainee to understand what they are asking him to do.

Verbal: A warm and positive tone in your best 'teacher voice' sends an underpinning message that you are confident and clear about what you want; therefore, you're far more likely to get a favourable canine response than if you share an inconsistent or half-hearted approach and vibe.

Visual: When teaching something new, it's often a good idea to marry up a hand signal with the verbal, as dogs often learn more quickly if both are used together consistently. If, for example, you've decided that putting your right arm straight up in the air will be your visual cue for 'Come,' then this action should be completed *every* time you give the verbal command. If the verbal cue is used and there's a delay before the visual is given (or maybe a hand is raised well before saying "Come") then these might seem like two separate events, potentially confusing your trainee and hindering the learning cycle. Practice giving any visual cue at the exact same time as the verbal—this of course applies to 'Come,' 'Sit,' 'Stay,' or any new behaviour you're trying to teach (*these commands are outlined in greater detail in future chapters*).

The main point here is to think about how we communicate with our trainees and strive to improve as teachers. If we become more self-aware, this will mean that any messages we send are likely to be clearer and will therefore be more easily understood. As a result, your trainee will love your clear and positive teaching vibe, develop confidence and progress quickly.

Body language

Many dogs have (at least) one PhD in human body language (!), observing us much of the day, every day, so if they are really good are gleaning meaning from how we present ourselves physically, we can use this to get the responses we're looking for. We should use warm and confident body language alongside our clear verbal and visual cues when interacting with and educating our trainees.

As mentioned already, self-awareness is important so we should pay attention to how we appear from our trainee's point of view. If you aren't behaving in a confident manner (both mentally and physically) and issue a half-hearted command to 'Come,' for example, you might be communicating too casually. Therefore, there's great scope in your trainee's mind not to take what you're saying very seriously, so do be careful about the vibe and messages you are sending. Making even subtle changes in how you appear just before you communicate verbally with your trainee means you're far more likely to have a successful interaction. By keeping your head up and shoulders back just before you calmly ask for a "Sit," for example, you're beginning with the underlying message that suggests you're 'in teacher mode' and are therefore more likely to be listened to. It's really important to remain relaxed and not stiffen up or become tense here—the point is to present yourself as a calm, positive and clear teacher ... determined to get your message across. When his bottom touches the floor, you could celebrate by crouching down and cuddling him affectionately while saying "Good Sit" excitedly for getting it right.

When training or interacting with your trainee, are there times you could change your own behaviour, body-language or appearance ... your vibe?

Keep it simple

A common problem with training is that we often try to progress too quickly and sometimes overwhelm a trainee, asking him to learn too many different things at once.

Remember, success breeds success, so try to teach only a couple of new behaviours at any one time and keep practising—little and often—until you're convinced these are pretty automatic before introducing any new ones. Keep training sessions simple and enjoyable. Integrating an active game—using a ball, a gundog dummy, frisbee or a toy, for example—into stationary 'Sit' and 'Stay' games is hugely important to the rapport that you want to foster and the positive vibe you want to share with your dog during the whole teaching/learning process.

Whenever you are schooling your trainee, try to make interactions fun, educational and brief ... and vary your approach according to the vibe he's sharing with you. If he's on top form then keep practising 'Sit/Stay' routines for a time, but if he starts slowing down or starts to get distracted when you're practising (and you feel this 'just isn't working very well right now,') then quickly switch to an activity that he's likely to focus on and enjoy. Definitely revisit what proved a little challenging later on in the training session (or soon thereafter) and strive for brief successes at that stage.

The message here is to keep a close eye on his vibe and react accordingly ... keep it simple. In this way, your dog will regard your teaching style as clear, fair and fun, and your vibe will be glowing from his perspective, keen to learn what you, his teacher, has to teach him next.

Try to avoid repeating commands

Reissuing a command over and over again in the same way, one that's being repeatedly ignored by your dog, is setting him up to ignore you again in future—not an approach that any good teacher (you) should practice. Try not, for example, to say 'Sit … Sitttt … Frankie, Sittt … for God's sake, Frankie, will you Sitttt downnn!?!' when asking your trainee to put his bottom on the ground. If you are having to make requests over and over, you're likely to fall into the frustration trap; your trainee might realise quickly that you're not feeling in control and decide to tune out your (negative) vibe even more at that stage. Provided you're clear that your trainee already understands the 'Sit' command (but is not really listening to you at the time), get his attention by calling his name and/or clapping your hands a couple of times exuberantly and, once you get his attention, say "Sit" *once* again clearly. When you get the responses you're looking for, always praise/reward using an upbeat vibe (maybe introduce a ball/toy or a game at this point too?) so your trainee is really motivated to want to repeat the behaviour.

Talking to dogs

Most of us, thankfully, have a very good idea about what is reasonable and what's not when it comes to talking to our dogs. Returning to your car after a walk in the woods on a rainy day, you might be overheard saying something like 'Come on, Max, get in there … OMG, look at the state of you! ... we're going to have to shower you off when we get home …' and this type of exchange is, of course, absolutely fine. Most of us don't need to change anything at all.

Some owners, however, can get into the habit of almost *constantly* speaking to their dog but, really, they should consider their vibe—how they appear from their trainee's perspective. Maybe they believe their words are comforting their pet in some way or perhaps feel the need to repeatedly connect with their dog by speaking. I'm not really sure. I'm certainly NOT saying, "don't talk to your dog," but I AM saying, "don't do this continuously." If you talk to your trainee all the time and always give your attention and affection *very* freely, you're simply desensitising him to the sound of your voice and your touch. Your (*very* frequent) affection and attention might become so familiar and automatic that these attributes are likely to decrease in value in his mind and you risk creating a situation where, when you ask him to do something or ask him to stop a behaviour, he might already have tuned out your vibe and 'your sound,' interpreting your words as just 'more of the same' he hears all day ... each and every day. For those constant talkers and touchers, please stop and think about the vibe you're presenting to your trainee.

So, if we want to present a 'good vibe' whenever we interact with our trainees, we should become more self-aware and practice having a positive and relaxed attitude/mind alongside clear facial expressions, a kind but determined tone of voice, helpful visual cues and confident body language—not to mention a bucket full of good common sense.

It's also crucial for any great teacher (you) to invest some time assessing/reading your trainee's vibe in different situations and remember, when training any behaviour, a good rule of thumb is to 'keep things simple' and progress steadily. It can be useful to look at how other people interact with their dogs too when you're out on walks and, if you meet someone you consider 'a natural' with their dog, try to learn from them and mimic their overall vibe and approach.

Finally, once you've really thought about the question, 'Is there anything I could do to improve my own vibe at home or when I'm out walking my dog?' ... do your best to make any changes in yourself re: 'how you feel and appear' from your trainee's perspective. Then practice 'being like this' around your trainee every day ... until it becomes the norm.

Chapter 2

Colours of the Mind

So, if *vibe* describes the key external feelings or energy we give off—and receive—whenever we interact with our dogs and vice versa, it would also be useful to have a system to refer to what's happening *inside* a dog's mind at any one time.

When considering a state of mind, a 'Traffic Light System' helps us share information more easily. Because of the visual nature of this system, people of all ages 'get it' and love its simplicity. It's really easy to understand, is very useful and works like this:

Red = Unbalanced/**Negative**

Amber = **Heightened**

Green = Balanced/**Positive**

Let's imagine your dog is casually playing with a favourite toy indoors and showing a pretty steady and 'cool' vibe—you might say he's presenting a relaxed or 'green' mind. If he's joined by another dog in your lounge and play quickly becomes fairly energetic, maybe even a little over-the-top, you might see some posturing or hear a low growl or two and observe 'amber' minds beginning to compete in front of you. If one dog gets possessive over a toy/ball and the vibe and exchange becomes a little too heated, the dogs might travel from an 'amber' to a 'red' state before too long.

- Sleeping = Green mind
- Aggression/fighting = Red mind
- Surprised by a sudden noise outside = Amber mind
- Panicking in busy situations = Red mind
- Mooching around the home = Green mind
- Running and playing in the garden = Green mind

When describing a state of mind, you might want to use 'low, middle and high' levels within each colour too at times. A dog could be anxiously 'high amber' just before a storm—beginning to pace and pant at home—but, when thunder strikes, he immediately goes into 'red' and darts to the bedroom looking for a quiet place to hide away ... it might take him hours before he reaches 'low amber' again.

I think, by now, you've got the general gist of the 'colours of the mind'! This system can and should be applied to us owners/handlers/trainers too, who should always strive to start and end with a 'green mind' whenever we interact with and train our dogs.

Reading vibe alongside colour

Please take a little care to weigh up the vibe you're getting *alongside* the colour of a dog's mind—sometimes a situation being evaluated might not be as straightforward as it first seems. In other words, try not to jump to conclusions too quickly.

Let's say that you've gone away camping in the countryside for the weekend and come across a stray dog who has very young puppies in a secluded den nearby. She might have raised hackles and signal aggressive growls and grumbles in your direction and to any other person or dog coming too close to where she's carefully hidden her pups. She might look quite aggressive and probably 'in the red' to most people and other dogs but, if a little time is taken to observe her movements and evaluate the colour of her mind, it might turn out that she's an experienced mum and secure in herself, but quite good at showing her strength and intention ... adept at putting on a good show while wearing a very calculating mind throughout. We might say—having observed her for a while—that she's "displaying a protective and aggressive vibe with a mid-amber mind."

You can see that it's useful to talk about 'vibe' alongside 'colour of mind' rather than separately, as each part offers great insight.

The 'vibe' and 'colours of the mind' system looks simplistic and it is, but please don't dismiss it given that it will prove really useful whenever we examine a dog's behaviour and try to speak about or analyse what's happening. Critics might mention that a 'vibe and colours' system is far too basic and subjective—where one person might describe a troubled dog's mind as 'red' and others might see it as 'mid amber.' Although this is a valid observation, also recognise that the system still gives us a good 'broad stroke' descriptive tool when referring to a dog's basic behaviour that we can use to share information and build conversations with others (while including other information too of course), so it is very worthwhile. We'll see much more of the 'colours of the mind' throughout this book and its usefulness will unfold but, for now, let's agree that the term 'vibe' represents the *vibration* you're feeling from and giving off to your trainee ... and a *colour* simply represents how you feel 'the mind is' at any one time.

What vibe are *you* sharing right now? Are you anxious, confident, content, excited, calm ... or ? How have your colours been today when you were around your trainee? What about other family members? What about your dog's colours—did these change at any time? What could you (and others at home) do to improve?

Chapter 3

Understanding Praise

We (humans) have discovered that we can accelerate learning by rewarding behaviours we'd like to see again. Praise gives us a way of making positive associations or links so, when we train a dog to 'Come,' for example, we immediately reward him for coming back when called. This will encourage our trainee to want to repeat the behaviour in future. Forging positive associations by praising or 'adding value' at just the right time is an excellent approach to use when teaching any dog.

How to praise

You can, of course, give varied food treats to your dog during any training activity and these can prove a brilliant motivator for many trainees, but it is very important to keep an eye on this and try not to over-treat using food. There are many alternatives to offering food treats and 'mixing up' how you praise is a great approach—reward with food (cooked chicken or ham, cheese etc.) at one time or give a cuddle (or both) sometimes too, or offer some animated handclapping and excited verbal feedback at times as well. Other common methods of positively reinforcing good behaviour might be to play a ball/toy game with your trainee directly after he's managed a successful 'Stay.' Some people simply let their dog off-lead to have some free time to signal they are delighted with what has just taken place. While we definitely should continue to use all of these effective methods of promoting good behaviour regularly, we should also think about our own body language, facial expressions and tone of voice when teaching and praising.

Body language and praise

Try to use your body language to praise effectively. By relaxing your shoulders and assuming a warm physical presence (maybe by bending down to your trainee or becoming more animated by smiling and clapping your hands excitedly, for example) is one simple way of demonstrating that you're delighted with him. Combining this approach with up-beat verbal praise ("Good boy!!") works very well.

Tone of voice

We can use our voices to praise effectively. Adopting a 'medium and high' system of feedback is a sensible approach here. Let's say you're teaching your dog to retrieve for the first time, for example … when he brings an item (a ball/toy/dummy etc.) back to you on command, you could use a very excited tone in your voice alongside welcoming body language and a special food treat (high value praise) to convey that you're over the moon with his behaviour. Once he's learnt a particular command and this has become automatic over a few weeks or months, you can gradually reduce your overall reaction to a medium level over time. If your lowered tones and reactions to a particular behaviour seem to be affecting performance negatively, then just go back a step, putting more energy and emphasis into your voice and body language to acknowledge that you're delighted with your trainee, and maintain this level of feedback for a longer time. Using your voice effectively and altering your tone at times is a fabulous motivational/signalling tool and one you should definitely use to your advantage.

Levels of praise

Please realise that, when you praise exuberantly, you are saying, "Yes, this is exactly what I want you to do! Brilliant!" If you ask your trainee Doug to 'Sit,' for example, and he pops his bottom on the floor quickly then you should reward this behaviour immediately with a hearty "Gooood boy, Doug!" or "Gooood Sit!! ... Clever boy!" alongside a cuddle or a game, or maybe a combination. If you only get a half-hearted attempt at the sitting behaviour you were hoping for or it takes much longer than it should, then offer praise at a 'reasonable' level (maybe using a simple verbal "Good boy" or "Good Sit") when your trainee eventually does what you are asking.

Some people reward every behaviour, often very low-level responses, *really* heartily. They want their trainee to be happy and feel good and really want to offer praise—but, if we think about it, this is not a very clear teaching strategy to adopt, particularly if you are not getting the behaviour or responsiveness you want. Don't confuse matters, even if your intention is kind. Simply match your level of praise to the responses your trainee is giving you. If you get low-level responses then offer slightly lower-level praise than you would whenever you see great behaviour, but *always give enough* to show you are pleased that 'he did it' … in the end! Whenever you get a very positive reaction/behaviour, or something very close to it, this is the time for sharing sincere, hearty and meaningful praise—lots of this.

Timing is key

Some dog trainers use Command, *A*ction, *P*raise (C.A.P.) as one way of helping owners remember the general system they should apply when beginning to train many standard instructions. For example, whenever you begin to train a new behaviour or command, you might issue an instruction like lay 'Down' (this is the *Command* phase) before guiding your dog into the correct position (the *Action* phase), followed immediately by a reward (the *Praise* phase) once the action has been achieved, i.e., *as soon as* the dog's chest/tummy is on the floor. Careful timing is so important. Offering the reward just as a dog's chest touches the floor makes the association in the trainee's mind that it was their chest making contact with the floor that the human really loved, so the dog quickly understands what 'Down' is all about. If your reward is presented a few seconds after the chest touches the floor, you are making it more difficult for your trainee to grasp what you are asking and the key moment may have passed.

Many of us are pretty good at carrying out the first two phases but sometimes we can forget to praise or we might move on too quickly to the next exercise before we really mark or acknowledge positive responses. Try not to miss any opportunity to fuel good behaviour and do this in a timely manner, particularly in the early phases of conditioning. Keep your positive vibe afloat and your dog will love learning ... and you, his teacher.

Nurture positive colours

While we already understand that we should 'reward and reinforce' good behaviour when training specific behaviours like 'Sit' and 'Come,' for example, an important message too is that praise can be used to fuel many other behaviours we'd like to see repeated in the future.

Some owners would be forgiven for seeing their high energy dog resting indoors and thinking 'Thank God for that, Sam's finally settled down ... phew! I hope no-one interacts with him, even looks at him—he might get up and drive us nuts all over again!' However, if we want a dog to relax and be 'green' inside the home or elsewhere, we might have to invest some time conditioning this behaviour to help convince him that being 'green' is a positive state, one that presents value/benefits. Praising any quiet behaviour—when he's resting, for example—by talking to him quietly or gently stroking or massaging your trainee's head or body for a few minutes or more, will encourage him to want to find that restful and contented 'green' state of mind as much as possible in the future and will help associate his bed and other areas in the home with resting and gaining your affection. As a result of these occasional nurturing efforts, you might find your trainee relaxing alongside you more often or laying in his bed regularly ... waiting for your 'green' attention and affection.

Later on, we'll explore attaching a word like 'Settle' or 'Relax' to this resting/green behaviour too but, for now, we should be aware that if we want a behaviour to blossom (like being 'settled' indoors), we should attach some value to it when we see it—by quietly praising/massaging/caressing at the right time—so our trainee is likely to want to do more of it! If we focus on nurturing green and low amber minds then these are the positive colours that we will see more of in the future.

Be careful not to nurture the wrong colour

From your dog's perspective, going out for a walk is regarded as HUGE praise/value for the behaviour and colour that came just before. So, if your trainee gets *really* stimulated before you both leave the home and this high amber state continues as you close the door behind you, he might be convinced that you went for a walk when, or even because, he got very excited/amber. If this is how he always feels and behaves when you leave home, he's very likely to do this again before the next walk and his colour will probably head in the wrong direction over time.

A more sensible approach to starting a walk might be to share a quieter, calmer and matter-of-fact vibe with your trainee. Your goal here is to communicate to your trainee, 'If your mind is green or low-mid amber (not over stimulated), I'll reward this vibe and colour by leaving the home and we'll go out for a nice walk' ... or you might think to yourself, 'I'll just wait until you improve your colour and behaviour a little more before I put your lead on and only then will we start to head off on our walk.'

Try to pay attention to the colour of your trainee's mind and focus on nurturing the colours and behaviours you want to see in the future.

Lavishing affection on the wrong colour

Let's say that your friend, Mary, has a Chihuahua called Charlie living at home, a very sweet-natured boy—a real looker—and loved by all his family members ... completely doted on by Mary. Charlie's life is great. However, he gets *really* frightened when he hears any fireworks or sudden noises, causing him to immediately fly into a panicked (red) state. His owners are lovely people and desperately want to help him when he's anxious so, if they hear fireworks going off, they quickly pick him up and cuddle him, taking turns to console him by stroking him non-stop and whispering sweet messages repeatedly to let him know that he's loved and nothing bad will happen, desperately trying to soothe his troubled mind. Mary doesn't sleep well at these stressful times as she worries so much about Charlie, who sleeps with her so she can keep a close eye on him and cuddle him. She repeatedly offers him treats throughout the night—which he never takes—but Mary's determined to try to change his focus and help him relax.

It's obvious that Charlie's humans mean very well—their intention is very positive and loving—but they are lavishing affection on (i.e., presenting great value to) a mind that's in the wrong colour. They are applying human psychology here and risk promoting this red mind/behaviour in their dog, even though their intention is to comfort. The next time Charlie hears a firework, he will almost certainly 'go to' that same shocked state of mind he was in the last time he heard the noise, given that constant affection/value was shared when he was in that state previously. There are so many different positive things Mary can do to help a dog like Charlie, including offering some gentle reassurance when he's in a stressed state (see *Chapter 36: Fireworks, Storms and Loud Noises*) but, for now, the key message here is to try to avoid *constantly* presenting HUGE value to the wrong colour, even if you are very well intentioned, as this approach might work against your goal of helping your dog improve his mindset and behaviour.

Capitalise on the 'good times'

As teachers, we should try to capitalise on three fabulous times in our dog's day to really motivate our trainees to want to learn. Each day we'll A) *feed* B) *walk* and C) *play with* our dogs so, about five minutes before each of these activities, why not do a little training?

A) If, for example, you want your dog to get good at the 'Sit/Stay/Come/Sit' game, simply prepare his food in his bowl and put it to one side. Let him see that it's ready. Then do the training routine for a few minutes—using a few treats at times—before finishing with some heightened verbal feedback and upbeat body-language ... then quickly give your trainee his meal. He'll be over the moon with his reward! He might see this as, 'I get super feedback and a whole bowl of delicious food for doing that new behaviour my human obviously loves—wow! I love this whole training thing!' You are going to feed him anyway, so 'seize the moment' and do some brief training (build responsiveness) before this key time.

B) The same concept applies just before you intend walking your dog. If you were to follow a short 'Sit/Stay/Come/Sit' practice session at home by instantly saying, "Okay, let's go for a walk," your trainee will be thrilled that one of the best rewards ever is being presented for being responsive to you, his teacher. This will only motivate him to be more 'on side' to any request in future.

C) Whenever you intend to play with a ball or favourite toy in the back garden or park, for example, appreciate that this presents great value for your trainee. Start by showing him that you have his favourite toy/ball/treat on offer and then ask for a few short (upbeat) 'Sit/Stay/Come/Sit' behaviours just before or within play. Repeat and repeat again! This process of 'learning in play' will really accelerate and cultivate great responsiveness in your trainee.

Think ahead and remember to 'add value' (i.e., reward green minds and good behaviour) in many different ways. It is said that 'Great trainers have great timing', so please focus on this when interacting with your trainee. Praise instantly and really meaningfully whenever you see great behaviour and responsiveness to you. Also, please teach others at home how to capitalise on the 'good times' in your trainee's day. Always nurture positive colours in different situations but remember to avoid 'lavishing affection' on the wrong colour and behaviour.

Do your best to fuel the teaching/learning cycle by being clear and encouraging so you can have a very happy, loving and responsive dog living at home.

Chapter 4

Guidance and Correction

Let's suppose a child started to draw on your walls at home, how would you react? Would you ignore what they're doing or maybe you would correct them and offer a little guidance so you won't have to see too much of that behaviour again in the future? 'Correction' is just that: mere guidance, a positive act—usually involving a swift verbal 'No' and 'Come over here' at just the right time—that conveys the message 'I am unhappy with your behaviour' or 'I'd prefer you didn't do that ... and please do this instead' and has nothing at all to do with any negative concept the word 'Correction' might initially conjure up.

When it comes to dogs, we already know that we can accelerate learning by praising our trainees to make our mutual interactions much more positive, but we should also appreciate that a little correction *is* appropriate at times, provided of course that your message is always delivered very fairly. A great mum nursing her puppies will often discourage youngsters from jumping up exuberantly on her, gently telling them off for nipping excitedly or biting her teats ... drawing a line in the sand when she sees a behaviour she regards as unwanted or unproductive or whenever a pup's colour moves into high amber or red. This natural teacher-dog/trainee-dog relationship must be taken on board by us as dog owners when trying to educate our trainees. Let's teach them to understand some simple boundaries and learn basic manners—enriching their lives and ours.

Ignoring unwanted behaviour

There are a few scenarios when it's appropriate, even necessary, to completely ignore a misbehaviour for a time. For example, let's say that Jackie agrees to foster Jerry from a local rescue centre for a month or so and, on his arrival home, she quickly realises that Jerry is a nervous wreck—his erratic behaviour indoors clearly suggests he's never been in a home environment before and he feels very unsure there. Jerry anxiously darts from room to room, panting, every sinew tense, living almost permanently in the red. In an effort to build up a little confidence, a short-term strategy Jackie could try might be to let Jerry explore the home environment at his own pace and let him investigate slowly, giving him time to come out of his shell and compose himself. His human carer could invest a lot of time and effort into 'staying green' and not putting any pressure whatsoever on Jerry, spending a lot of time *not* giving him too much attention unless he seeks contact or interaction. Even if Jerry wees or poops in the house or reacts neurotically to the television, phone, radio or vacuum cleaner, everything is ignored. This can help him realise over time that nothing bad is taking place and he can gradually move down into amber and, eventually, green.

Aside from certain specific cases like Jerry's, ignoring bad behaviour can be a passive and often a very slow method of changing existing misbehaviour. If, for example, your dog always jumps up on you frantically at the front door and consistently gets really excited with visitors, you might be advised by some owners/trainers/behaviourists to follow an 'ignoring and turning your back on him' strategy whenever you arrive home. The idea is that, if he's quiet and respectful, he is acknowledged and praised; if he's being a hooligan, he gets ignored. This strategy is designed to give your dog minimal feedback/value while in a mid/high amber state and, in time, motivate him to improve his behaviour the next time you or a visitor enters the home. In my experience, some dogs can learn good behaviour (over time) if they're taught like this, but many others will just keep practising exuberant 'jumping up' behaviour and get really good at it as the days and weeks roll on ... and then these behaviours can become more engrained and take longer to turn around.

Rather than ignoring poor behaviour, why not consider having a simple system of presenting the 'I like this' vibe' to your trainee at key times and 'I don't like this vibe' sometimes too? ... using a very balanced and informed teacher-like approach. Definitely use a few treats and toys to redirect and refocus the mind at key times as this approach can also be very helpful. Your trainee will learn what you want quickly through your guidance and not by having to somehow 'figure out' what behaviour you are looking for through trial and error.

Timing

If we look back at the C.A.P. method of training a dog, timing is obviously key to the question, 'When should we praise our dogs?' When we say 'Sit' and our trainee is (hopefully) very responsive, we should offer hearty praise *immediately* we see his bottom touching the ground, to reinforce what we want to see again.

It's also crucial that we try to catch and respond to any misbehaviour as early as we can, never allowing things to escalate and then decide to correct later on—by which time it might prove more challenging to sort things out. Whining or barking indoors is one example of behaviour that's frequently ignored in the early stages, as a dog often starts off using low whining/barking sounds and these can be quite far apart. If you have a dog that whines/barks at home or in the car regularly and he 'isn't too bad' on a particular day, you might mistakenly think 'Phew! ... that's a lot better than yesterday' and not bother to address any (minor) sounds immediately. Or worse, you might say, "Good boy," after a few low whines—trying to acknowledge the improvement in his behaviour—but really end up telling him that the sound he's making is okay, even welcome. When your trainee then decides to really 'go for it' and whines or barks in a determined manner (moving into high amber), it's far more difficult to motivate him to stop than if we'd said, "No" when this behaviour was being expressed in a low-key or low amber manner. As you can see, timely reactions from the teacher (you) are very important.

Durations of time

Scientists tell us that dogs are very good at making links or associations between events, provided these take place in a short time span. If you open the cupboard/larder door and your trainee hears you removing his food bowl and preparing his meal, some hope or expectation of being fed will definitely present itself. If you feed your trainee straight away and repeat the process daily, the link between 'larder door opening' and 'being fed' will quickly strengthen.

Scientists also note that, while dogs can learn associations quickly, the time frame or duration of the behavioural process must be quite brief for strong links to be forged. If, for example, you open the larder door and your trainee hears you removing his food bowl and you then repeatedly forget to feed him until an hour or so later, the association or link won't be made between 'larder door opening' and 'being fed' or, if the link is present, it will be weak.

Because our trainees think in the 'here and now' and only 'join up' events if these are close together, it is very important to factor this into our thinking when we return home to find 'a certain someone' has peed on the carpet an hour or two earlier. If a dog is scolded with a firm "No" for a misdemeanour that happened some time ago, this approach is very unlikely to be understood by the trainee. If you were able to interview your trainee, he might recall events as: 'human left home… I waited for ages … not much to do … peed indoors … ate a spider … waited some more … barked at people passing by … human came home … human was very angry and ranted (a lot) … I have no idea why I was being scolded …' For a dog, it's likely that events happened too far apart to be able to 'make the link' between peeing indoors and being told off hours later. To avoid a situation where a trainee might be told off for something he doesn't understand and is left feeling very confused, please bear in mind that dogs find it difficult to associate ideas that are far apart in time. We must all be green teachers and always very fair to our trainees, focused on building positive relationships and avoiding any confusion or breakdown in communication.

Verbal correction

The most automatic method of correction for most of us is through verbal communication. By making a very clear sound, deliberately formed to show we're unhappy with a specific behaviour, we can quickly get our point across. Some people use a sharp 'No' or 'Ah-Ah' sound. Try to choose a short disapproving sound that comes automatically to you or make one up that feels quite comfortable for you. Ideally, everyone at home should be consistent and use the same sound, so your dog clearly recognises that particular human 'noise' as 'NOT happy.' What is your 'NOT happy' sound?

By keeping your verbal communication brief when addressing a misbehaviour, any frustrations will not be as readily transmitted as if you were to start an exchange by saying things like, "For God's sake, Sparky, what *is* wrong with you today? Just listen to me! LISTEN!" Stick with clear and simple sounds, trying to keep a green/calm demeanour as much as possible. Your trainee is, of course, likely to tune out any half-hearted feedback so a confident and persistent approach is a 'must have' throughout. Issue instructions and any corrections or praise so they sound like you mean them.

If you're having trouble influencing your trainee using verbal corrections alone and he's clearly not listening to you, the combination of clapping your hands quickly a couple of times at the same time you say, "No" or "Ah-Ah" usually gets the message across, particularly if he's nearby. You should consider integrating some of the following methods into your correction repertoire too, so you'll have a range of strategies up your sleeve should you need them.

Body language

As mentioned earlier, our dogs read our body language very effectively so we should use this to our advantage. Let's say that your dog, Kiko, is a chewer at home and you've just caught him munching on your favourite shoes or on a piece of furniture! Placing one or both of your hands on your hips is a position that makes you look more imposing from Kiko's perspective, signalling clearly that you're not impressed with what's taking place. Making a sound like "Kiko, no" at the same time reinforces your clear message: 'NOT happy.'

Eye contact

We rescued Missy, a wonderful black German Shepherd, from GSRE (http://gsrelite.co.uk) when she was around three years old. Missy had some serious behavioural problems in the beginning—problems we worked through and solved—and while she led a very full and happy life, sadly, she recently passed away aged eleven years. She comes to mind here as I remember her as the 'queen of eye contact!' As an older girl with some lower back problems, she really disliked any over-excitement (other dogs running or jumping around nearby) when we were out on a walk—probably fearful of getting jumped on or against, as she knew this could prove painful. If another dog became very excited around her when out on a walk she would often stop and stare for a moment to make the clear statement: 'I am aware of an excited vibe and behaviour ... NOT happy.' She might also have postured in a slightly tense manner and even given off a low grumble, which supported her visual message. If the excited behaviour eased, Missy would often avert her gaze a little and relax her body language—maybe smell the ground or have a wee—to signal that she was now more content, given that the other party's behaviour was heading in the right direction. If the excitement was revisited, then her stare and posturing were too, more intently this time. Once the excited behaviour had been curbed, the teacher's gaze was again averted as her body language relaxed and she would then happily meet the other dog and they would always get along famously.

As your dog's teacher, you too can apply a similar method of giving (brief) strong eye contact to your dog to display disapproval. This message can be enhanced even further if you combine any strong eye-contact with a verbal 'Ah-Ah' or 'No' sound alongside assertive body language.

What to do when any misbehaviour stops

Soon after your trainee gets the message and stops a misbehaviour, you must react accordingly, as another dog would, and back off from the situation. Let things 'cool off' for a short time. Please don't say "Good boy" as soon as your dog stops barking, for example—even if your intention is to communicate you are delighted that he has finally stopped—as you risk telling him, 'I am pleased with you,' and this might only start the barking behaviour off again. Wait for about 30 seconds or so of good, quiet behaviour after a correction before inviting your trainee to come to you for some positive contact. It's vital that you stop and WAIT for a quiet period after a correction before you interact very positively, so the message you're teaching and sharing is clear: I was unhappy with what just occurred but now I welcome the green mind and listening vibe you are sharing.

Silence is powerful

Many of us might be guilty of disagreeing with a behaviour by saying something like, "No, Freya, stop it ... I said stop it ... Freya, noooooo! What did I just say? Leeeeeeave it!" And it might not stop there. When we use lots of words, the message can sometimes be lost on our trainee. So, a better strategy might be to say, "No" or "Ah-Ah" once or twice firmly, alongside confident body language and then ... say nothing at all. The lack of many different words can be quite influential here—you might find that your trainee listens to you far more when you simply say less. Sometimes the combination of a green 'teacher mind,' a clear brief verbal message, some strong eye contact alongside a little posturing and some deafening silence will win the race. Silence *is* powerful—try using it just after correcting at key times and see how effective this approach can be.

Your lead is a control tool

Depending on a range of factors, your trainee might not pay attention to your verbal correction, eye contact, confident body language or even your best combination, so you might find yourself in a position where you have to think of another approach. Some older dogs may have very well-established (bad) habits and are just doing what they've always done; so please be patient here and try not to get bogged down in your 'usual correction method' that doesn't seem to be having much of an effect on your trainee. Consider using your lead more—particularly indoors—as one means of regaining control at key times, to help guide your trainee and keep him in a positive/reasonable colour.

Let's suppose that Jamie, a large dog, lives at home with you. He loves it when guests arrive and gets really excited—practising a mid and high amber mindset—particularly for the first five minutes or so, spinning and jumping around, breathing very heavily, barking excitedly and making everyone's lives uncomfortable ... and probably getting very mixed feedback from all. One strategy to counter Jamie's very excited behaviour might be to practice putting a lead on him indoors when there are no guests or stimulation present, getting him used to settling down alongside you at times each day. If you make a cup of tea, you could put Jamie on his lead and ask him to "Settle" or "Relax" calmly beside you. Cuddles can and should be given at times (calmly, of course) provided Jamie remains green or low amber. Jamie can sit or lay down or move around a little during the session but he shouldn't pull on his lead. Avoid offering treats during this exercise as these won't really help

Jamie find a relaxed state of mind. We will explore this strategy further in the 'Dog Yoga' section (see *Chapter 15*), but the basic approach here is for Jamie to practice having a green or low amber mind indoors and to get really good at it by doing this on-lead 'waiting routine' a couple of times each day. Then, on the day your guests arrive, place a lead on Jamie before you answer the door, ask your guests to have a seat and relax for a few minutes while they avoid speaking to or interacting with Jamie for a very short time. During this period Jamie should be alongside you in this familiar position, (hopefully) waiting fairly patiently and getting some positive input and affection from you ... and definitely not making the whole room feel uncomfortable, given that someone is now guiding/leading. After a few minutes or later on, when you feel the time and colour is right, let go of the lead or take the lead off Jamie and say very little—just a simple 'Good boy' or 'Good Settle' for being calm and to reinforce that you are happy with his colour and behaviour.

Using your lead to help manage situations indoors is a really worthwhile tactic, particularly in the initial stages of training/educating as you can take control of situations quite quickly, well before a mind finds a negative colour. This is very relevant if you have a high-energy trainee that regularly gets really excited or unruly at home when visitors arrive. Puppies and young dogs can really benefit from this 'Settle routine' too. Having a lead easily available in the home requires a little forward thinking and planning—maybe you could keep one in your lounge and another by the front door?

Avoid correcting and then praising straight away

As mentioned previously, occasionally we might—with the best of intentions—make the mistake of combining correction and praise, which can prove really confusing for our trainees. Let's look at a scenario ... James and Michelle have a large Briard called Tolli, a sweet soul that everyone regards as 'just amazing' and is a treasured member of the family. James has to work away for a few weeks and upon his return home, buys the most fabulous coffee table for Michelle, something she's really wanted for some time. Michelle's delighted, the rest of the family are delighted, even the neighbours have come over to see the fabulous table—they all love it too! Over the weekend, Tolli starts to investigate the 'new item' in the lounge and before too long ... a gentle nibble and, yes, you guessed it ... it gets worse! James and Michelle hear the frantic scratching noises and quickly run into the lounge only to find one of the table legs ... along with the rest of it ... in bits. James shouts at Tolli, "You naughty dog, mooooove, get away Tolli, AWAY, you baaad dog!" Tolli realises his humans are definitely not happy and darts away quickly. Michelle then says, "Good boy, Tolli" in an attempt to mark or acknowledge the fact that Tolli moved away from the table when asked and she was very keen to soothe him after James shouted at him so aggressively. Later in the day, Tolli went back to investigate the table remains and James saw his approach and, furious, really shouted at Tolli again.

If Tolli was to 'write in his diary' that evening, the entry might look like this: 'James brought a fancy table home and after a while I went into the lounge to take a closer look.

Okay, I did eat a chunk out of one of the legs but, as soon as I heard James screaming at me, I stopped and moved away straight away. Clearly, he hated me eating the table leg. Then Michelle told me several times that I was a "Good boy." I was convinced they meant "Ok, we didn't like you eating the table a few seconds ago but now it's fine." Later in the day, thinking all was well, I went back for a closer look and got a real telling off ... my humans are so confused—they don't know what they like and don't like ...'

So that we're always kind and fair to our trainees, we must be careful to issue only very clear messages. The vibe we share must be unambiguous, i.e., this teacher 'does' or 'does not' like this behaviour. In a situation like the chewing example, saying a firm 'Tolli, No' and 'Leave' alongside confident body language is usually enough to get your message across, but let's be clear that any combination like "No, Naughty Tolli" followed quickly by "What a clever boy, Tolli" is not a great way to deliver the message 'I don't like this' or 'NOT happy.'

Fairness

As mentioned earlier, 'Correction,' if presented fairly, is simply 'Guidance' and is a very important tool in the whole teaching and learning process. A timely verbal 'No' or 'Ah-Ah' is usually enough to deliver a disapproving message. As good teachers, we must cultivate a very positive teacher/trainee relationship and strive to stay green whenever we are around our trainees and avoid situations where amber human minds might surface and negativity creeps in.

Effective use of your voice, body language and eye contact are all great tools to use when showing you are not very impressed with a particular behaviour. Being silent for a short time after a verbal correction can be influential too. If you're consistent and your timing is prompt, the level of energy you'll have to invest in guiding and correcting your trainee will reduce dramatically very quickly, by which time your attention will be focused almost entirely on praising positive behaviour.

Chapter 5

The Value of Exercise

Just being together while having a great time exercising outside the home is sure to increase the bond and understanding between you and your dog. No doubt about it. It's really vital that we get each trainee out and about every day as this will help develop his physical and mental health, his socialisation skills and increase his confidence in the outside world. Owners who exercise their dogs well on a daily basis often notice very positive behavioural differences and increased responsivity in the home as a result—these can be very marked, particularly if you have a high energy trainee.

Your dog's exercise needs

Common sense tells us that a high-energy working breed is likely to need more exercise than a low-energy or older dog. Trying to establish what is 'a good amount of exercise' therefore becomes difficult to prescribe, as this varies between younger and older dogs, breeds and even among littermates. Try to follow the general guidelines issued below and tailor the amount and type of exercise to your individual charge.

One key point to make here is that some owners fall into the trap of thinking that their small dogs—because of their size—do not need very much exercise at all, feeling that walking around the home or garden is 'more than ample for their little legs.' No. Many smaller dogs can have quite high energy levels and sometimes need lots of stimulation both inside and outside the home if they're going to be content. So, please remember that your small dog *is* a dog and has associated needs. Some (large and small) breeds *need* to run and burn off some steam if they are going to be satisfied, while others are very content to amble alongside on a walk before heading home to relax on the sofa for hours at a time. The core message here is to know your breed and your individual dog and tailor your exercise regimes accordingly, trying to ensure your trainee's exercise and stimulation needs are met.

Also, if you've more than one dog living at home, it's very important to exercise your trainees together on a daily basis or as often as you can. Some very well-intentioned owners say things like, "We took Darwin out for a walk yesterday because he really needed it," leaving another, often quieter or slightly older, dog behind. Regularly taking one dog out and not another can potentially affect the vibe at home and might fuel some canine rivalry and divisions, so care needs to be taken here. While, of course, we occasionally need to separate our dogs because one needs to go to the vet, a bitch is in season or a dog is injured or elderly and needs short walks or some 'quiet time,' we should acknowledge that (most) dogs living under one roof will benefit greatly from the experience of walking outside together as one unit, as much as is practically possible. If you have more than one trainee at home and don't feel able to walk all of them by yourself, ask other family members, friends or a professional dog walker to walk with you—each person walking one dog, for example—so all your trainees get to move outside at the same time. If this isn't possible every day, then maybe walk them individually at times and try to get them out on a group walk a few times a week or as much as you can.

A general guide

So, what does a sensible exercise regime look like? People often have very different opinions here but two stimulating walks per day, each lasting *at least* half an hour, is a good general rule of thumb for adult dogs. This routine could be followed up with a short walk around the block and/or some 'wee-time' in the garden in the late evening so your trainee can have a comfortable night. This is really the *bare minimum* requirement for most healthy adult dogs to be satisfied—if you can do more, so much the better. If your trainee is going to be stimulated outside of these exercise sessions by giving him regular access to a garden or an outside area as well, then great. If, however, your system of 'two walks per day' is the only exercise provided, you will need to increase the exercise durations already suggested, so your trainee gets enough stimulation outside the (very familiar) home environment.

Puppies often benefit from adopting the 'little and often' approach to exercise where they go out for a walk for, say, ten or fifteen minutes at a time and do so a few times a day, gradually extending/varying this as they become stronger and more confident. Do limit the amount of exercise any young dog gets—remember, they are growing fast.

Also, please don't just allow dogs to 'get on with it' at home if you see high-amber youthful canine minds bounding and bouncing around in front of you for long periods. You are their teacher, so feel free to 'stop interactions' at times ... some juveniles are unlikely to stop themselves and can easily overdo it. If you have a large or giant-breed puppy, take extra care when exercising, as these often have specific exercise guidelines—doing too much when these puppies are quite young can be very detrimental. Please check with your breeder or vet, who will be able to advise what kind of exercise is most relevant and how much to offer your puppy as he matures.

'Free' exercise

'Free' exercise is 'unstructured,' meaning your dog exercises without too much direct interaction with you, his owner/teacher. A trainee might be taken to the beach, park or woods to drain his energy levels by sniffing around, chasing squirrels, playing with other dogs and generally having a blast. This is a very common and very useful form of exercise, where dogs are largely 'allowed to be dogs' and they certainly love it. While you might feel that you're playing a fairly passive role here much of the time, you're definitely seen as the provider of the walk and associated with the great events of the day.

'Structured' exercise

This is where you communicate more closely with your trainee during exercise time, motivating him to do certain things and praising him as he does them. Both owner and trainee are in sync, focused on the same activity or goal. For example, you could take your dog out for an on-lead walk in town and ask him to focus on your movement and follow your lead—walking nicely alongside while stopping and starting, crossing roads, turning left and right, occasionally practising 'waiting alongside' while you meet and speak with people. Once he has practiced walking well on-lead, you could then find a safe off-lead exercise area and ask him to "Wait, Sit, Stay," (see *ESSENTIAL COMMANDS*) before throwing a ball, followed by "Find it, Come, Drop it ... Gooood boy." These should become automatic communications for anyone engaging in some structured exercise with one or more trainee. At first, this method of exercise might appear a little controlling from your point of view, but if the regime is presented by an interesting and upbeat teacher (you), inventing new positive challenges and experiences as you walk, your dog will really love it.

Another example of structured exercise might be to practise some heelwork (walking nicely on-lead) for a short time before using a few 'Sit/Stay/Come' commands and then deliberately dropping a ball/toy on the ground while saying, "Leave it" at the same time. Encourage your trainee to walk forward alongside you on-lead for twenty or thirty metres or more, maybe using a food treat to lure him forward and keep his attention. Once you get far enough away from where the ball/toy is, give the food treat—provided your trainee's colour is positive—and, pointing your dog in the right direction, remove the lead and send your (excited) trainee off to retrieve the item using an exuberant 'Find it' command and follow this with lots of praise on his return.

Then think about giving your trainee the 'Free-time' or 'Break' command and let him have some freedom and some unstructured playtime. In this way, you will make a great link with the earlier heelwork experience.

These structured/responsive activities that you dream up will catapult you into the realms of 'great teacher' from your dog's perspective and he will be physically and mentally challenged. He'll certainly be more content and will become more responsive and bonded to you as a result. What kind of games will you use to help stimulate and train your dog?

Both at the same time

Ideally, free and structured forms of exercise should be used alongside each other daily. Applying a routine where around half the total exercise time is focused on free exercise and the other half on structured activities is one very good approach. Please use good common sense here, allowing a certain amount of exercise initially to drain energy levels before asking your trainee to practice stationary activities like 'Sit' or 'Stay,' for example. Enjoy your exercise time—be buoyant, have fun and your trainee will love it too.

Having a very good exercise regime in place helps develop sound communication skills between trainer and trainee, and provides so many other benefits—dogs who get 'out and about regularly' tend to be much easier to live with at home. It's always useful to think about any changes or improvements you and other family members might make to your trainee's existing exercise habits and act on these. Maybe you and others at home can you do a little more training (e.g., 'Sit, Stay, Come, Fetch' etc.) or game-playing throughout the day ... or a family member might volunteer to do a short 15-minute on-lead walk each evening to add to your existing exercise routine? Over time, any extra daily stimulus—if offered routinely—will really enable your dog to practice 'being green or low amber' more often in the home.

ESSENTIAL COMMANDS

Chapter 6

Your Approach to Training

Even a very basic understanding of what we want our dogs to do in certain situations will greatly enhance their lives and ours. Every owner should invest some time educating their dog, young or old, practising 'Sit,' 'Wait' and other key commands on a 'little and often' basis, so both human and canine can get along really well through a mutual understanding of simple words and behaviours that will be used in everyday life.

When should you start?

Begin training your commands today, whatever age your dog is, but do take it slowly. Make sure you step into your positive teacher role when training and have fun—lots of it. Be clear and consistent so your trainee will love your approach to teaching him ... and you for taking the time to do so. Will you train in the garden or in the park, on a walk or maybe you intend setting aside specific training times daily? Hopefully, you'll try all of the above. Think about what you want to achieve in the short-term, maybe over the next two weeks, and write down a few small and achievable goals. For example, you might decide that you want your young dog to know how to 'Sit' and 'Stay' (a short distance away) by a certain date—this will help give you some focus.

Patience is key

Try to plan ahead and concentrate your efforts on training one or two new commands at any one time until these are really in place, almost automatic, before adding any new behaviour to your training syllabus. Think about how you will share information with your trainee so you can communicate clearly, making it easy for him to learn. Try to be aware of your trainee's age and his progression to date, as well as the complexity of what's being taught and alter your teaching strategies accordingly. 'Being patient' in training is a key attribute—with your trainee and with yourself.

Clicker training

A clicker is a very small and simple mechanical device—one model/design looks a bit like a small key fob with a button on one side—and it makes a clear 'click' sound when you press it. The noise is very consistent and can be a great means of signalling to your trainee that you are very happy with a particular behaviour.

Start teaching your dog the 'clicking' game by holding your clicker and, if he's wearing a green mind, 'click' *once* right next to him. When he looks at you, say "Good" or "Yes" excitedly straight away and give him a tasty treat. He doesn't have to do anything at all for the treat at this stage—except look at you and 'share a moment'—as we just want him to listen and make a simple association: 'Click = Approval.' Wait for 30 seconds or so and 'click' again (once) and immediately reinforce the 'looking at you' behaviour by saying "Good" or "Yes" as you treat him. Practice like this for very short periods—a few minutes at a time—and condition your trainee a few times a day for a couple of days. Please don't over-click! He is likely to love this 'free treats' game and will quickly get the idea that each click means you are pleased with him and that 'special noise' always sounds just as something really nice happens. Once some basic conditioning is clearly in place and he is really keen on the new 'clicking' sound, the idea is that if you are teaching your dog to 'Sit' and he pops his bottom on the floor, you should immediately 'click' to signal that you are delighted with what he has just done and then say "Good" or "Yes" as you give him a treat. The reward must be given *as soon as possible* after the click, making a wonderful association. Each click marks good behaviour and represents the message, 'Well done, you!' You can use your 'click and reward' system with any behaviour you want to foster.

Clicker training will suit some people more than others but it is worth considering, particularly if you are very softly spoken or your verbal reactions are a little slower than you would like or if your trainee is already used to tuning you out and you need a 'fresh approach.' Also, if there is some inconsistency at home with regard to how different family members interact when training a dog, then a clicker can be part of the solution—if everyone at home uses one to reinforce good behaviour, particularly in the early phases of training, your trainee will get very clear and consistent feedback which will definitely help him learn quickly. Young people at home can really benefit from using a clicker too—this tool is likely to improve timing and consistency in any young trainer and make learning easier for your trainee. You will need to show young people how to use the clicker effectively, of course—explaining and emphasising the importance of timing and 'marking' good behaviour *as soon as* they see it. A clicker can be a useful ally, so, if you think this tool might suit you and your trainee, consider integrating it into your teaching strategies.

Short bursts

Training (with or without a clicker) for a few minutes or so followed by a game or some exercise, repeated a few times a day, is likely to be a far more positive and productive experience—for trainer and trainee—than trying to engage a dog in an intense training session lasting half an hour or more. Rather than setting a twenty-minute training guideline, for example, think instead of embedding your training session within a twenty-minute game. You could take Tamu, your trainee, into the back garden with three or four toys and share an enthusiastic "Tamu, do you want to do some training?" before getting started by throwing a ball/toy that she can fetch. After a few successful retrieves, you could place a lead on Tamu and ask her to "Sit" and "Stay" just before throwing or maybe hiding the ball again. After waiting for a minute or so you might take her lead off and send her after the ball with a motivational 'Find' or 'Fetch' command. You get the idea.

Once your dog becomes familiar with short everyday obedience routines like 'Sit/Stay/Find/Come/Drop it' you can start extending the amount of time spent schooling your trainee. But do this gradually, sensibly gauging when to call a training session off.

Knowing when to switch

If an occasion crops up ... and it might ... where you feel that training is not going too well, the golden rule is to stop practising the exercise (quickly) and switch your focus. Find something your dog does well, like 'Stay' or 'Fetch' and do this for a short time. Evaluate why a particular training session didn't go to plan or wasn't as productive as it used to be and think about what you need to change ... then practice again the following day with a very positive and green mind. As teachers we obviously need to be fairly persistent in training at times, but knowing when to call a lesson off or when to quickly switch from instructional to game-playing mode is an attribute worth perfecting. This 'switching' ensures that negativity is never allowed to creep very far into any training experience.

Finish on a positive

As you complete any training session, however brief, make this clear to your trainee by saying, "Free time" or "Break" or "That'll do" or something like this. You could clap your hands twice excitedly/quickly too just as you look at your trainee when finishing any training 'game' or come up with your own method of signalling: 'Thank you, game over!' Remember to praise heartily at the end of each training session with upbeat interactions using a few treats and/or a short game of 'tug' or 'fetch' (or both), motivating your trainee to really crave being very responsive to you in future.

Some key points to note …

- Start teaching straight away, but take things slowly
- Only teach one or two new commands at any one time
- Be patient with your trainee (and with yourself)
- Embed training within game playing
- Have fun and, if things are not going to plan, switch!
- Finish each training routine by saying something like "Free time" or "Break" exuberantly and follow this with a treat or a short game, so 'listening to you' always presents great value
- Be very positive/green throughout any training session and try to get really good at reading your dog's feelings/vibe as you progress
- Also, try to evaluate *yourself* throughout each training session too, so you improve your teaching skills over time

Now that we have a good idea of how to approach training in general, we can identify those key commands we should all teach our dogs early on. The following section describes how you can teach six essential commands—those you're likely to use daily: *Sit, Wait, Stay, Come, Nicely/Gently and Close/Heel.*

Chapter 7

Sit

Put your bottom on the floor

Search for ***LoveK9 TV*** *on YouTube to view our* ***Sit*** *video*

Environment

When schooling any new behaviour, think about where you will do much of your teaching—your lounge, back garden or a quiet area of the park are all suitable venues when training 'Sit.' It seems like an obvious point to make, but try to avoid training in noisy or stimulating environments or you will make it hard for your trainee to concentrate and learn. Build up strong associations and good habits first in quieter areas and then you can raise the bar a little and practice in the park, for example, once your trainee knows exactly what's required.

Using a lure

While there are a few different ways to teach the 'Sit' behaviour, one very effective way is to use a suitable lure to keep your dog's interest—a juicy treat, a tennis ball, a favourite toy or a combination of these is bound to work

well. Consider using a verbal cue alongside an appropriate visual cue—your verbal command will be an enthusiastic 'Sit' and your visual cue could be an underarm movement, as outlined in these images.

Start by positioning your trainee so he's standing in front of you, preferably looking at you. Place the lure—treat or toy—in front of your body near your dog's nose and keep him focused. Then, with the palm of your hand facing upwards, move your hand (with the lure) slowly from just above his nose and push it over his eyes, making sure to keep the lure very near to his muzzle all the time. As a result of moving your hand over his face, your dog's nose and head will naturally move upwards and backwards, following the lure. If you think about your dog's physical makeup, you'll see that this 'up and backwards' head movement will automatically help tip or guide his rear end towards the ground.

<u>If your trainee is alongside</u>

If your dog is right beside you, it's important to use the same verbal and visual cue he is already familiar with and try to avoid moving your feet at all—focus on moving your arm and upper-body only. If you start moving your feet so you can face your dog, he will probably start to move around too and it will take longer to get the 'Sit' behaviour you are looking for. So, if your trainee is on your left-hand side, cross your right arm over your body and move your right hand (with the lure) over your trainee's face. Once your trainee pops his bottom on the floor, give some instant positive feedback.

<u>Timing is key</u>

Timing is very important in any training activity if you're going to be really clear and make learning easy, so try to praise your trainee *as soon as* his bottom touches the ground by giving the lure straight away, making the connection in his mind that 'Sit' means 'bottom on floor.' A reward might involve a hearty verbal 'Yes' or 'Good Sit,' a toy, treat or short game … a combination of these will work well.

Pushing your dog into the 'Sit'

One older training method advises placing a hand on your dog's rear end and pushing him into position while saying "Sit" at the same time. While this approach to training can work fairly well when your dog is on-lead and near you in the home, it has drawbacks. Firstly, you are 'pushing' his bottom to the ground so there's a feeling of pressure here ... not a great start ... and secondly, your trainee is likely to learn quickly that when you're not near enough and he's off-lead, he doesn't have to listen to you—he knows you can't push him into position. Instead, try to stick to the lure training strategy as much as you can and condition your trainee to be responsive to your verbal and visual 'Sit' signals, whether he's near you or at a distance from you.

Strong links

Rehearse 'Sit' throughout the day at different times and do so just before you play a game with a ball, before your dog gets fed or goes out for a walk and just before allowing him off lead. From your trainee's perspective, doing the 'Sit' behaviour starts these great events, so you are cultivating a really positive association here. Before long, he should automatically 'Sit' whenever he hears the word or sees your hand signal.

Whistle conditioning

Once your trainee is quite responsive to your usual 'Sit' command, you might find it useful to attach a whistle sound to the behaviour too. Simply ask your trainee to "Sit" (using your verbal and visual cue) and follow this up *immediately* with your whistle sound—this is normally a single 'screeching' peep on a whistle to signal 'Stop, Sit and Listen.' If you follow any positive response to the new sound with something your dog really loves to do and use high-value food rewards at key times, you should have a whistle-responsive trainee alongside in no time at all. After a short time—a few weeks—your trainee should be so familiar with the system (when you are practising at home) that you can start using the 'Sit' whistle sound alongside your visual cue—no verbal cue is required—and, very gradually, increase the distance involved. Later on, provided you are getting great responses at home, you can start practising the new 'whistle behaviour' in quieter areas of the park too.

Overusing 'Sit'

Once Mylo has learnt to 'Sit' on command there's a real danger the instruction can become overused at home. Almost every time some owners communicate with their dog, 'Sit' is in there somewhere: 'Mylo, can you Sit down?' or 'No, Mylo, just Sit over there,' or 'Don't do that, Mylo, Sit down ... just SITTT!' We don't want a trainee being told to 'Sit' so much that he becomes desensitised to the word—we need to be fair, so some basic house rules should be agreed upon among adults and any young people at home. The key message here is to use the 'Sit' instruction sparingly but try to ensure your trainee does sit down when you use the word. Don't forget to immediately praise positive behaviour.

Chapter 8

Wait

Relax with me

Horse riders/trainers understand the importance of having a relaxed connection between a teacher and their equine trainee. When lunge lining a horse, schooling him to go clockwise and then asking him to change direction, it's very important to maintain a relaxed line connecting the handler and trainee most of the time. This approach is sometimes referred to as keeping 'a smile in the line;' in other words, making sure there's no tension in the line connecting trainer and trainee. Once a relaxed line becomes the norm, the horse realises that he's doing the exercise well and harmony exists. As soon as there's no smile in the line, he's instantly aware that this tense and less comfortable state means that something isn't quite right.

Similar thinking can be applied to dog training, where the 'Wait' command simply asks a dog to stop and relax with you on a smiling lead, i.e., without any tension, until you decide to move off again. 'Wait' conditions your trainee to look for 'no tension' in his lead and to keep that smile in the line as much as possible. So, exactly how can you train your dog to 'Wait' and keep your lead smiling?

Environment

As mentioned already, start training any new behaviour in an area without too many distractions initially—your back garden or a quiet area near where you live is fine—so your trainee can concentrate on what you're teaching him. Once he has the idea and is doing well, you can start practising the new behaviour in busier situations as well.

Exercise first, then train

If your dog's pretty active and you decide to take him to the park to practice the 'Wait' game, fantastic; but think about stacking the deck in your favour here too, so you're more likely to have a successful training session. Let your trainee burn off some calories before asking for any waiting behaviour—by giving him a good walk or run beforehand you will encourage a more relaxed and receptive mind on the other end of the lead and you'll achieve your educational goals more quickly.

Visual Cue

Some owners help their dogs learn the 'Wait' behaviour quickly by introducing a visual cue alongside the verbal. Some prefer to point at their dog as they say "Wait" and then invite him to come in for some cuddles while 'waiting.' Others use a 'splayed hand' held in one fixed position (*see pic*). Having a clear visual cue in place will really help the learning cycle, so think about what yours will be.

Lure training

Have a lure ready—a few small pieces of cheese, cooked chicken or a favourite toy will be ideal ... then put a lead on your trainee and start walking. After taking a few steps, ask your trainee to 'Wait' and quickly push the lure out in front of you near his nose—he's unlikely to move too far away from the lure and all the time he'll be keeping a smile in his lead. Once the lead has been smiling for about ten seconds, give him the reward to mark a responsive 'Wait' behaviour and follow this quickly with a hearty, "Gooood Wait." The next time you want him to 'Wait,' present the lure again and invite him to come *right into you* to get it, thereby generating a smile in the lead. If you repeat this process your trainee will quickly get the idea that 'Wait' means 'remain green on a smiling lead' and good things follow.

Tension

Be really clear in your own mind that when you say "Wait," it means your trainee should stop and wait with you without any tension in the lead. If he only pulls a little bit after being asked to 'Wait,' don't fall into the trap of thinking 'Oh, that's not too bad' or 'that's an improvement' and say nothing. Instead, say, "Ah-Ah" and "Wait" again whenever you feel the lead get taut. This communicates the clear message that 'Wait' means 'NO tension in the lead please ...' as opposed to 'A little tension is fine.' When he's stopped and waiting correctly, praise in the usual way by saying, "Gooood Wait" and follow this with lots of affection.

When to use 'Wait'

Once you've taught a steady 'Wait,' remember to use your cue as you approach the end of a footpath or as another person and dog approaches you in the street, when you leave or return home with your dog and also just before your trainee gets into or out of the car. As you can see, this is a really useful control tool so try to perfect it as soon as you can—puppies and older dogs usually pick this command up very quickly indeed so you'll reap great rewards straight away. Before long, you'll be able to use the 'Wait' command to ask your dog to stop and relax with you when he's off-lead as well.

His lead is usually smiling
But sometimes just a grin
My teaching sometimes soaring
And other times quite thin;
But overall I do believe
The bond we have is sound
Between me, my family and
Our faithful, hairy hound.

Caroline Roberts

Chapter 9

Stay

Don't move out of position

*Search for **LoveK9 TV** on YouTube to view our **Stay** video*

'Stay' asks a dog to remain in one position and introduces the notion of putting some distance between you and your trainee. You'll move away from him and then return as part of the 'Stay' routine, as opposed to asking him to 'Wait' alongside you. The 'Stay' command can be taught using various techniques but the most straightforward method assumes that a dog clearly understands the 'Wait' behaviour before attempting to train 'Stay.' Once a steady 'Wait' has been mastered, it's a good idea to involve a family member or friend to act as a volunteer, informing them about the 'Stay' routine you're going to rehearse together and the supportive role they must take on.

Starting correctly

Find a quiet spot in your back garden or a park and start walking around with Luna on-lead while you practice the 'Wait' and 'Sit' commands a few times. Ask your volunteer to walk around with you too. Then hand over Luna's lead to your helper and get them to ask her to 'Sit' and 'Wait' in one position while facing you. Once Luna is sitting alongside your volunteer and focused on you, make a clear hand gesture towards her while saying "Stay" at the same time. The common 'Stay' hand gesture is a splayed hand where a trainer's fingers are outstretched and the hand is pushed towards the dog at exactly the same time as the verbal instruction is given. As mentioned already, it's important that the two (verbal and visual) signals are issued together at the same time, so please focus on this. When you say "Stay" and make the hand gesture, your volunteer must immediately ask Luna to "Wait." No-one should talk to her at this point as it may motivate her to move out of position. Then back away from Luna, just a few feet initially. Provided she's remained stationary, return to her after only a short time—about five to ten seconds or so in the very beginning—and both you and your helper should promote good behaviour by saying, "Good Stay" heartily while giving affection and a couple of treats. Try not to get her over excited with your praise, otherwise you risk convincing Luna to get really charged up when you return the next time—not a behaviour you want to encourage. Reinforce the command by repeating the exercise a number of times, very gradually extending the duration of the 'Stay' behaviour and the distance you move away.

Go back to your dog

Avoid calling a trainee already in the 'Stay' position to you. Instead, always return to Luna to praise a correct 'Stay'—particularly in the early stages of training—and remember to use your visual cue as you return to her. If she gets accustomed to coming out of the 'Stay' position and moving towards you—because you called her to you—Luna might start predicting being called during the staying phase and choose to travel towards you of her own accord. Returning to your trainee consistently (in the early phases of training) conditions a very steady 'Stay' behaviour. Later on, when your 'Stay' routine is perfected and Luna knows exactly what's required, you can start using the 'Come' command to call her out of the 'Stay' position towards you.

Wait before praising

Once Luna understands the basics and can 'Stay' consistently for very short periods, when you return to her in the 'Stay' position, practice standing beside her quietly for about three seconds before rewarding. The whole 'Stay' routine, from Luna's perspective, will then become very clear—you give the 'Stay' command, walk away from her, return to her, then you wait for a short period before completing the exercise and rewarding her. This short waiting time before you acknowledge good 'staying' behaviour on your return tends to stop a trainee getting overly excited as you return and will create a far steadier 'Stay' than if you reward just as you come back.

Try not to let your trainee fail

Once you've mastered 'Stay' from a few feet away, don't be tempted to increase the distance too much too quickly, as this may cause anxiety in your dog's mind and possibly jeopardise a successful exercise. Be a patient teacher. Remember, each time you try this or any training activity, you must do your best not to let your trainee fail the exercise. If this means that you have to repeat the exercise a number of times at the same distance, day after day, then so be it. That's far better than trying to achieve too much too soon and then having to start training and conditioning from scratch again. Many people can get impatient and/or very ambitious once they see a little progress, so do guard against this. Increase the distance you move away from your trainee very gradually day-by-day.

If Luna does move out of position at any time, either you or your volunteer must address this immediately with a brief 'Ah-Ah' before repositioning her calmly and starting the exercise again. Try to keep verbal interaction to a minimum during a 'Stay' exercise but do remember to use your splayed hand signal quite frequently during the early stages of training and whenever you return to your trainee. As soon as you've had a few successes engage Luna in some play-time while sharing a very positive vibe.

Use your lead effectively

Once your trainee clearly gets really good at the 'Stay' routine you can start to practice without your volunteer. With Luna on-lead and in a 'Sit' position, give the 'Stay' command and back away a pace or two while facing her, still holding the lead while making sure it doesn't go taut. Don't move to the end of the lead at first but ease your way to the full length of it only after a number of successes. If Luna moves out of position, then immediately say "No" or "Ah-Ah" and start again using your 'Stay' command. Practice for short periods only. After a couple of successful training exercises, offer Luna a stimulating diversion such as a game with a ball before restarting.

Pendulum approach

A variation on the previous training technique is one we call 'the pendulum approach,' which conditions a dog to remain in one position while you stand in front of him before 'swinging' or walking to either side of him, moving a little to his left and right.

Simply give the 'Stay' command while facing your on-lead trainee. Take a couple of short steps backwards from him in a straight line, facing him at all times, particularly in the early stages of training. Then give the 'Stay' command once more and reinforce it using your hand signal at the same time. Move a few paces to the right of your trainee while holding the lead,

keeping it smiling. Return to the position in front of your dog, again asking him to "Stay." Then move to the left a few paces and 'swing back' again so you're just in front of him. Finally, go back to him and stand beside him for three seconds or so before praising him for being a star and completing a really great routine.

Then take a break and allow your trainee to walk or run freely if possible and change your focus away from 'Stay' training for a short time.

Revisit your 'Stay game' regularly until he's quite relaxed with fairly random movements away from and around him and the whole process becomes very familiar. Try to avoid saying "Stay" every couple of seconds, opting instead to give a clear hand signal or a single verbal "Stay" command if you want to reinstruct. Build up your confidence—and your trainee's—through short repetitions daily and consider using a long training lead too, so that you can maintain additional control while the behaviour is being taught.

Build steadiness first

You can develop the pendulum routine further over time to include walking around behind your dog, completing full circles around him, but please be patient as your trainee needs to build up his confidence. When you increase the pendulum motion to the point where you're about to walk/swing behind your trainee and you're in a blind spot, be aware that he may get up and move ... to keep his eyes on you. Pushing things too far too quickly here is likely to mean that a successful 'Stay' exercise is jeopardised. Take your time and build steadiness first before getting too ambitious, particularly if you have a young or energetic dog or one with a very inquisitive mind.

Out of sight

Once you are seeing very consistent 'Stay' behaviour at close quarters, why not start to gradually increase the distance involved and then (later on) include some 'out-of-sight Stay' behaviour too? Begin at home by asking for a 'Stay' and then leave the room for a moment, before returning very quickly and rewarding. Work up in small increments, extending the amount of time you are 'out of sight' from a couple of seconds to five, then ten seconds or longer. After returning to your trainee, remember to wait for three seconds or so and then give lots of praise and engage in a game or some free time. If you need some support here, ask a family member or friend to keep your trainee on-lead while you practice the new 'out-of-sight Stay' behaviour and, after many successes, gradually work up to being able to train on your own.

'Stay' games

Playing games that use the 'Stay' command is a great way to teach and reinforce good behaviour, however, this is only advisable once your dog is already very steady in the behaviour. You could ask your trainee to "Stay" for a short time while you hide an article in another room or in the garden … then return to him and wait three seconds or so before saying "Find" excitedly—this kind of interaction will make a great association with the 'Stay' behaviour. Be inventive about what you choose to hide—some treats, a toy or a ball are all good tools—and give a fair amount of thought to where you will hide the items. Make it easy for him to find the goodies at first and then gradually increase the level of difficulty and lengthen the duration of the 'Stay.' Before too long your trainee will crave playing these brilliant 'Stay' and 'Find' games.

Chapter 10

Come

Come back to me

Having a dog that responds very well to the 'Come' or recall command is a must for all dog owners. The usual way to call your trainee is to use his name followed by the 'Come' or the 'Here' command. Some owners also help a dog learn what's required by adding a visual cue just as they say, "Bracken, Come." This could be an arm outstretched straight up in the air or to the side, or some people stretch out both arms either side of them (see *pic above*) each time they give their verbal "Bracken, Come" or "Bracken, Here" instruction. You must choose that verbal and visual cue which feels right for you and, as mentioned earlier, please focus on using these at the very same time if you're going to appear clear and consistent from your trainee's perspective.

Thinking ahead

Many trainees will not come back immediately when called because their natural inquisitive side takes over when they're 'out and about', so we should try to stimulate them and reduce their energy levels a little before we take them out 'in the open' to practice recall. If we start training a dog after being exercised in the back garden with a tennis ball or after some on-lead heelwork or both, we're much more likely to get a positive response when we call him. This is a much more sensible approach than practising recall with a trainee who is completely fresh and supercharged. An important point to understand is that each successful exercise generates more success so we should try to nudge the probability of success in our favour early on by thinking ahead.

Two-step recall

Try to think of the 'Come' command as a 'two-step' process, where the first part asks your trainee to come to you and the second asks that he expects to be touched lightly and briefly on the neck just before being rewarded. Having the second step in place avoids the common scenario where a dog responds well in early training routines and returns to you every time, but later on might develop a tendency to move in your general direction when he hears your "Come" command but, just as he gets back near you, then heads off to do his own thing ... a very frustrating 'game' for owners.

High-value rewards

Let's imagine you're twelve years old and you go off to a friend's house for a sleepover. Soon after arriving, your friend Jane tells you excitedly that her mum and dad have just come into some money. 'Good for them,' you think to yourself. After some time, Jane's mum calls you both into the kitchen and, just as you get there, she smiles and places a few notes on the table. Jane's mum excitedly says, "You two can keep those ... all of them." You and Jane are over the moon and both run and pick them up straight away. Later on, she calls you both into the kitchen again—once more holding a bundle of notes—and gestures in your direction to come a little closer. As you both hurry towards her, she lays a few on the table, once again saying, "You can have these." What do you think your reaction will be the next time Jane's mum calls your name?

If you want to make a really great association with the 'Come' command, then it makes sense to go for very high value rewards particularly in the early stages of training. These can be phased out later on. Some dogs will be very responsive to food treats, so ham or chicken treats are a good idea. Most will really *love* liver cake and cheesy bites (see the sample recipes outlined at the end of *Chapter 16: Using Food Wisely*). Many trainees will even leave a play session with other dogs to return to their owners when called if they think the 'extra special' treat might be on offer. Once you've experimented a little and figured out what high-value food treat or particular toy will motivate your trainee to perform well, then a good strategy would be to use particular rewards only when recall is being practiced. So, the *only* time your trainee will ever taste those extra special food treats or get that particular 'super-toy' is when he returns when called, giving the reward in question even greater value in his mind.

So, now that you know to use a verbal and visual cue, and get the general gist of the 'two-step' recall process and have thought about what you might use as a high-value lure for your trainee, how should you train the 'Come' behaviour?

Stage 1

Find a place with very few distractions to help Bracken focus on learning—a garden, an enclosed tennis court or a quiet area in a field will be ideal. One good approach when training is to ask someone else to help you, particularly in the very early stages. A family member, a friend or neighbour—familiar to your trainee—will be good choices. Once you're ready, begin the exercise by walking Bracken on lead around the area. Ask your volunteer to walk alongside you and, after a few minutes, hand over Bracken's lead. Ask your volunteer to say "Sit" and "Wait" to Bracken while you move a short distance away—around four or five metres or so initially. Once he's sitting nicely beside your volunteer, face your trainee and make it obvious that you have a treat or toy on offer before walking another couple of metres away from him. Your volunteer should maintain control, saying "Wait" again whenever necessary. After a very short time, face Bracken and use your excited "Bracken, Come" command alongside your clear visual cue, giving off a very welcoming vibe. Once Bracken's clearly focused on you, signal to your volunteer to release him or run/walk him towards you. As he comes to you, repeat the verbal "Bracken, Come" command and push the toy or treat out in front of you. Encourage him to move right into you for some brief contact, reward very affectionately and quickly give him the toy or treat.

Stage 2

Making contact when he returns to you is very important, by touching him gently or holding his collar lightly for a second or so, but never grabbing it quickly. If you're consistent here the 'two-step' process will become routine in his mind—hearing the 'Come' sound means to move quickly in your direction before being touched lightly on the neck or gently held by his collar for a moment. Only reward once contact has already been made, communicating the clear message that the 'Come' exercise is completed only when you touch. Then release him for a brief play session by saying, "Free-time" or something like this. After a little playtime rehearse the 'Come' behaviour again, this time moving further away from him (just a little) before calling, touching and praising.

Vary your routine at times

You can develop your recall system to become a two-way process too, where your trainee runs between you and your volunteer a few times. If both of you use a selection of toys, balls or food treats to reward successful 'Come' commands, you will really motivate your dog's interest and performance in training. It's also useful to vary your routine, placing your trainee on-lead after a recall sometimes and releasing him with a 'Free-time' instruction at others. This means that he'll never know if he is coming back to you to be given a treat and put on-lead or told to go and play.

Practising on your own

If you're training the 'Come' command on your own, then it would be ideal if you have already trained your dog to 'Sit' and 'Stay.' Get a few high-value treats or a toy you know your trainee will really love and practice indoors or in your garden initially. Start by asking your trainee to "Sit" and "Stay" just before moving a few metres away. Then, facing your trainee, focus on using an excited verbal cue like "Come" or "Here" alongside a strong visual cue—maybe by stretching your hands/arms out in a welcoming manner. Make brief contact when he returns to you, asking him to 'Sit' and tell him excitedly what a "Gooood boy" he is and give the reward immediately. Try to get family members to practice too, so your dog learns to 'Come' to everyone rather than only the chosen few. After a few days of this level of training, start to increase the distance between you and your trainee—very gradually—provided you are happy that he 'gets the idea' and is already very good at coming back to you from a shorter distance.

A dynamic approach

In addition to practising these very useful 'recall drills', you might like to explore a slightly more dynamic training routine at home too. Choose a few high value treats or toys and go out into the garden or enclosed area. Then start by asking your trainee, Beano, to "Sit" and quickly throw a single treat/toy while saying "Beano, Find" excitedly. Just as he picks it up, call him to you again enthusiastically with an upbeat, "Beano, Come!" If he comes right into you, make light contact quickly on his neck area and immediately throw treat/toy number two in a different direction, again saying, "Beano, Find" eagerly at the same time. After five or six treats/toys have been picked up (i.e., short successful recalls have been completed,) give him lots of praise and then shift your focus away from 'Come,' leaving Beano with a mind that wants 'lots more of that' ... and feels like: 'wow, that was exciting!' Remember, when using this strategy, there is no waiting time when your trainee returns to you—simply touch his neck/collar very quickly before throwing the next treat or toy to be retrieved. If you do your best to be a very dynamic and motivating teacher, this 'Come' game will become a very exhilarating one to practice and your trainee should get very good at being responsive. Practice 'little and often' and always reward heartily.

Training leads

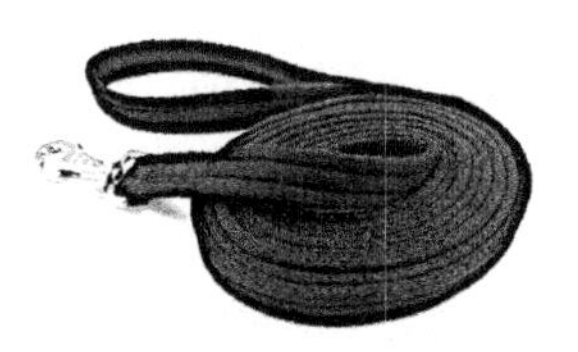

Many people, particularly those who've already experienced negative or inconsistent recall responses, could start training a steady 'recall' at home using a long training lead—sometimes called a 'trailing lead' or 'recall line.' If you don't want to buy a ready-made one, visit your local hardware shop and get around six metres of thin rope—the thickness you select should be in keeping with the size of your dog. Fasten this to your trainee's collar securely and get him used to having it trail on the ground behind him while investigating your garden or an enclosed area. Of course, you should never leave your dog unsupervised while wearing a long training lead as it can easily get entangled in garden or park furniture, trees, shrubs and other objects, so please use good common sense. Practice on open ground where any snagging won't occur. Your long line will mean you have a lot more control of your trainee and, hopefully, much more success in training and conditioning as a result.

If you're doing some training in the back garden and have given an excited "Come" command but your trainee hasn't come back to you and is clearly in his own world a short distance away, stand on the end of the long line and say "Come" again excitedly. If there's still no positive reaction then take hold of the end of the training lead and try to get his attention by clapping your hands together quickly while calling him exuberantly. You should avoid any 'pulling' on the lead here as this will only associate a negative feeling with the 'Come' command, which is not what you want. Simply hold onto the lead, restricting where he can go, and reissue the command using a very welcoming and excited vibe and by showing him the lure—really motivating him to come to you. Remember to make light contact with him on his return and reward him as he does.

After a few weeks of conditioning good recall behaviour by using the long line in the back garden, once your trainee is pretty consistent, start using it when walking in quiet areas outside the home too. Hold the end of the line all the time you are practising 'Come' outside the home, at the same time giving your trainee a little more freedom. After another few weeks of solid conditioning, depending on how he is doing, consider going to a quiet area of a park (with some toys and high-value treats) and drop the line on the ground, so your trainee is 'free' but has the line trailing behind him on the ground in an open space. Continue on your walk as you would normally, as though nothing much is taking place. Maybe it would be a good idea to ask a friend to join you for these first few 'off lead' walks so you have some support alongside—choose someone who will help you stay green and positive.

Other dogs can help

Walking with other people and their dogs can also help to tip the likelihood of training success in your favour, particularly if you have friends with dogs who have excellent recall skills already. Dogs who walk/run with others when out and about will often come back alongside those who have more reliable recall habits, particularly if there's a fabulous reward presented on their return—one trainee won't want another to get all the goodies! These walks can provide excellent training opportunities so try to find someone to work/walk with if your dog needs some practice.

If he comes back but takes his time

If your trainee is off-lead and doesn't come back to you immediately when called but does return after a while, it's important not to scold him. You might have to dig deep here to avoid giving off negative vibes, as you may well have been waiting and worried for what seemed like ages for a positive response. But recognise that he *has* come back to you, so you must try not to make a negative association here. A very old training mantra goes something like, 'Whoever scolds a dog who returns will only convince him to take longer to come back next time' and this still holds true today. At these times of 'slow return,' simply praise by saying "Good boy" briefly when your trainee does return and put him back on-lead. Then ask him to "Wait" and you should take a minute (or more) to breathe deeply! Try to stay green and continue walking. Your medium level praise and vibe will signal that you are 'mildly pleased' with his behaviour (given that he did return ... *eventually*) but you are making it clear that you are not very impressed with his performance levels. Revisit the long training lead technique that was mentioned earlier in a more controlled environment—like your garden and an enclosed park—for a couple of weeks or so to recondition what's expected. Avoid letting your trainee off-lead in a stimulating environment again until you have regained your confidence that he will return when called.

Don't overuse the recall

In order to maintain and build a positive association with the recall instruction, try not to overuse it and fall into bad habits like calling your dog to you excessively when out on a walk. Some owners go to the park and, right from the start, insist their trainee remains almost beside them the entire time saying things like, "Ringo ... Come ... Come ... Ah-Ah, Ringo ... No ... Come over here" every few seconds. If Ringo is pretty high-spirited, you really are fighting the tide here, so use good common sense and give him some freedom *before* you practice your first recall. If you're patient, you might even find that he comes back of his own accord (having had a look around) to see if you have anything interesting like a tennis ball, cuddle or a tug-game to offer. If this happens do reward Ringo's 'coming back to you without instruction' behaviour straight away by finding something 'valuable' and interesting to do, so this 'positive you' will be the vibe he'll expect when he returns again following your next recall.

Reward recall with 'Free-time'

When training, remember to nurture good 'Come' behaviour by praising *very* energetically whenever he returns to you quickly (showing your trainee how much 'returning to you' means to you) and follow this with a 'Free-time' or 'Go play' instruction regularly too, so this 'going back to the human' behaviour really pays off. Your dog will be delighted with a system that teaches: "Come" = Return quickly, get a few tasty treats from an excited and delighted human, a cuddle and maybe a game ...and this often ends with lots more freedom!

The whistle

Some dog owners have a very reliable verbal recall behaviour at home and in other places, provided there aren't too many distractions around. If, however, you're in the park and there's something vaguely interesting on the horizon, behaviour patterns can alter. Some trainees develop instant selective hearing and you might find that your verbal "Come" is being ignored. When dogs are stimulated by lots of activity and are not coming back when called, they're often not really being disobedient but the sound of our voices may not register with them, particularly if they're engrossed in a fabulous activity like rabbit hunting or playing around with other dogs.

Gundogs and working/pastoral breeds are normally particularly responsive to whistles but most dogs respond quickly, provided you invest some time making the positive association with the sound at home first, before relying on it outdoors on a walk. A consistent whistle sound presents a number of benefits. Firstly, it can often reach and penetrate a trainee's mind much more effectively than our voices, particularly if he is some distance away. Secondly, the whistle can be passed around among family members (or you may decide to purchase a few whistles) so your trainee hears the same sound from all family members. Also, a whistle creates a sound that doesn't show frustration, concern or represent any other emotion that might be revealed if you were calling your trainee. Lots of whistle types exist but a basic plastic gundog whistle—an ACME gundog whistle, for example—is a good choice.

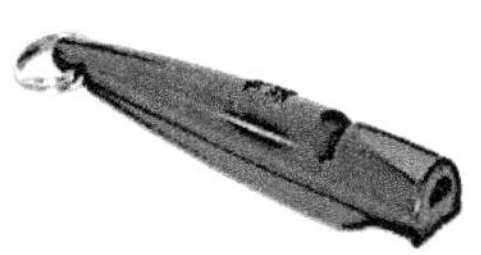

How to practice

Three short whistle 'peeps' in quick succession is an appropriate sound to make whenever you want to signal the 'Come' behaviour. Try to use your familiar visual cue alongside your whistle sounds and be consistent here. Regularly use your whistle indoors to call your trainee to you, particularly just before you feed him, before you put a lead on to take him out for a walk and before you play with a favourite toy. In this way, the new sound signals that something wonderful is about to happen—the only thing your trainee has to do is to go to you to find out what it is, creating a very curious and positive association with the whistle sound. Provided you're quite confident that you have a reliable recall in the home, try using the whistle in the garden on occasions and then progress to a quiet area outside the home, making sure that you reward the 'two-step' recall using positive verbal feedback, a game, toy and a super high-value food treat. Ask a family member or friend to help you practice and apply the same recall techniques outlined earlier—think about giving your volunteer a whistle and a few tasty treats or toys too when practising the two-way recall.

Whistle conditioning

Please set aside some time daily to condition your trainee to come back to you every time he hears the whistle sound. High value food lures and any toys your trainee really loves are your allies here, particularly early on. Once you've conditioned a very responsive behaviour at home, which might take a few weeks or longer, you can then start to practice whistle training outside by going to a quiet area of the park or beach with a friend, *gradually* building up your experience and confidence levels—and your trainee's.

What will your next training session look like? Will you exercise your trainee beforehand? Where will you practice? Would you like someone else there? Will you involve another dog? What treat and toy lures will you use? Are you planning on using a training lead and a whistle? Thinking ahead when training will really help.

Chapter 11

Nicely or Gently

Be gentle with your mouth

As well as steering clear of any activities that might promote mouthing or 'teeth on hands' behaviour at home, it's a great idea to teach the 'Nicely' or 'Gently' command to show your trainee how you would like him to behave with his mouth. 'Be gentle with your mouth' or 'teeth on hands are not welcome' is the central message this command conveys.

The routine

Ask Dolly to 'Sit' in front of you, preferably on-lead, and show her you have a treat in your hand. Make a fist (with the treat), upturned. Then place your fist near her nose and, while relaxing your fingers slightly, use the 'Nicely' verbal cue to signal there's something on offer, but please be very clear that her approach needs to be respectful in order to get the reward. Try to keep your hand still, in one fixed position—don't pull it away or wave it around during this exercise as any sudden movement might

stimulate Dolly's mind and trigger some excitement. Her nose should come up to and over your fist to investigate the treat, while you say "Nicely" a couple of times. Wait a few seconds at least and, provided her vibe and approach are gentle, open your fingers further and allow her to take the reward, at the same time praising the correct behaviour by saying, "Gooood Nicely" in a very upbeat tone. Your relaxed hand alongside the gesture of giving the tasty treat signal your obvious approval too.

After practising this new behaviour for a time, whenever Dolly hears 'Nicely' and sees a hand/fist extended in her direction, you might find that she investigates the hand briefly and then simply takes her nose away from it, clearly showing that she now knows the game! 'I'm being polite' is the message she's sharing. If this happens, offer the treat immediately and give verbal praise to convey 'Brilliant ... this is exactly what I want.'

If the approach is full-on

If your trainee's vibe is too busy or disrespectful and you are being pawed frantically or you feel teeth pressing against your fingers, then keep your fist clenched and in one position but say "Ah-Ah" to signal that you don't approve of this approach and show that you never promote the wrong colour. Continue practising and reward any positive approach by treating and adding lots of verbal reinforcement. Once your trainee's been successful a few times, stop schooling this behaviour and maybe revisit your 'Nicely/Gently' exercise later in the day, always striving to end your brief and upbeat training interactions on a very positive note, leaving your trainee with a mind that 'wants lots more of that!'

Promote good behaviour, not improved behaviour

Always avoid giving a treat if Dolly is using her mouth too keenly or is not behaving in a respectful fashion. Remember that treats are used for rewarding good behaviour and a positive colour, so avoid telling yourself, 'Well, that was an improvement from the behaviour I saw yesterday,' and end up rewarding what's really incorrect behaviour. There's a saying: 'What you pet is what you get,' which means if you are rewarding excellent behaviour, then this is what you will see more of. If you are praising behaviour that isn't quite right (even if it's better than before), then this is probably what you will get in the future. Try to remain consistent, making sure that you send crystal clear messages to your trainee to encourage swift progress.

Young people at home

Young people will benefit greatly from being taught how to behave in situations when, for example, they are giving their dog a treat. Making sure they have a clear 'system' to apply means they will be more confident and appear more consistent from your trainee's perspective, which will greatly enhance behaviour.

You'll need to show youngsters exactly how to stand, how to hold and give a treat, what they should say and how to say it, explaining how important it is that any excitement or screaming should always be avoided. Teach them about colours of the mind and make a game of it. Use questions like 'What colour are you right now?' and 'What colour do you think I am?' and 'What about Jake?' to get your message across. Show them a variety of fun routines to follow too—a basic routine might involve asking Jake to "Come ... Sit ... Nicely" and giving a treat. Then, use the 'Stay' command before placing a treat in the distance and saying, "Jake: Fetch ... Come ... Sit ... Nicely" while offering another treat alongside verbal praise. These rehearsals will result in a greatly increased sense of confidence in young people and your trainee, so you should see improvements in both human and canine behaviour almost immediately.

Young people, of course, always need to be supervised when around animals, so the first thing they should be prompted to do if unsure about any situation is to ask for your help or the help of another adult or an older sibling at home. Good common sense is vital here. If you have a dog that's fairly casual with his mouth and maybe even nips occasionally, then youngsters should NOT practice this command/routine at all until the dog has been schooled by adults and then only after he's reliably behaving in a *much* gentler manner.

Hand feeding

It's a fabulous idea to hand-feed some of your trainee's food regularly too, particularly if he doesn't have a naturally soft or gentle mouth, so you can educate him about what is acceptable behaviour and what is not. A sensible approach, particularly for any dog with a very keen appetite—one who is 'a bit too eager' to get to a treat—is to feed him (just a small amount) before you practice. Then, with keenness of appetite a little subdued, engage him in a number of activities like 'Sit, Stay, Come,' while asking him to take each piece of his remaining food 'Nicely' from your hand.

Revisit your routine throughout the day, every day, until you're achieving the respectful approach you want. In this way your trainee is consistently getting the message that being gentle with his mouth presents great rewards and any other behaviour results in the absence of any value ... no treats or affection for a short time. If your approach is clear, your trainee should respond positively and learn quickly—only using his mouth in a very gentle manner in future.

Chapter 12

Close or Heel

Walk nicely beside me

Walking any dog that pulls you forward on-lead and weaves left and right whenever he wants, randomly crossing over in front of and behind you, is clearly quite dangerous and not a behaviour we want to foster. Any trainee behaving like this will almost certainly trip his human walker up at some point or, at the very least, make the whole (daily!) walking experience very stressful for everyone. This random 'pulling and weaving' behaviour is one you could curb by schooling your trainee to know how to walk correctly on-lead. Having a very clear 'walking system' in mind will really help you teach your trainee what kind of behaviour you are looking for. Let's start by exploring three types of walking accessory that might affect your progress when walking your trainee.

Retractable Leads

Retractable leads, extendable leads, wander leads and flexi leads are different names for this device. This particular lead has a plastic handle housing a spring-loaded mechanism that allows the lead to be pulled out (i.e., extended) by your trainee when out on a walk, giving him a certain amount of freedom while you maintain some control too. The lead/line also retracts easily, automatically gathering up inside the plastic handle without too much effort on the part of the handler. This is a really useful tool in many situations. It's fantastic if you want to practice recall or if you're visiting Aunty Helen for the weekend—for example, if you are walking Thor in unfamiliar territory and looking for an opportunity to let him stretch his legs in a local park/field or maybe you have a female dog who is 'in season' and want to exercise her safely away from other dogs.

However, do consider using this tool sparingly when beginning to train a dog to walk correctly on-lead as they can often encourage a trainee to pull for more freedom rather than achieve a relaxed mind alongside his handler when out on a walk. If Thor pulls repeatedly on a short retractable lead that's 'locked' (i.e., fixed and not extended), in order to get a break from the frustration resulting from Thor's never-ending pulling efforts, some very kind and well-meaning owners might easily think 'Oh, go on then, you have a little run' and press the release button to allow him to move forward to the full extent of the lead. As you will appreciate, this (human) behaviour presents value at the wrong time … and will condition Thor to repeatedly pull on-lead, always trying to get his owner to press the 'magic release button' for more freedom. Certainly, do think about introducing a retractable lead later on, as they can be invaluable in many situations, but really consider schooling your dog to walk well on a standard fixed lead beforehand … or maybe you could use different leads at different times?

Harnesses

Harnesses are used effectively by tracking dogs when engaging in scent-work, allowing them to pull forward to a scent while affording them a great amount of freedom when sniffing the ground or air. Sled dogs are strapped into harnesses so they can put the full power of their bodies into any pulling motion and Guide dogs work in harnesses for a variety of reasons—so there's no doubt that harnesses can be very useful in various situations.

Manufacturers of dog accessories often promote 'No Pull Dog Harnesses, Front Clip Vest Harnesses, Dog Car Harnesses,' etc. and customers can choose from varieties like 'Padded, Reflective, Breathable and Lightweight.' Some manufacturers emphasise that their particular type of harness will teach a dog not to pull, while distributing any pressure more evenly around his body and taking a great deal of strain off his neck and trachea, keen to make the point that harnesses offer a safer and more comfortable alternative to the standard lead and collar. So, assuming your dog, Lewis, already practices a strong pulling action on-lead, rather than see him strain at the neck or hear the unpleasant snorting sounds he makes on a walk, you could quickly arrive at the obvious notion that a harness will really suit him—the logic being that a harness will provide extra comfort for him when out and about on a lead and any snorting noises may stop too. Excellent. If Lewis walks nicely on a harness and you feel like you have enough control, then that's great—you don't

really need to change anything. Keep using the tool that clearly works well for you and your trainee.

If, however, Lewis loves the comfort of a harness and uses it to pull you all over the place and doesn't really listen to you very much on a walk, it might be sensible to consider using a standard collar and lead, in the beginning at least, to teach Lewis how you want him to walk properly before going back to the harness later on if you want to. For those owners of a brachial breed (i.e., a dog with a short head/muzzle) where breathing issues might be a concern on a lead walk, you might like the idea of using two leads at the same time, at least in the short-term. Connect one lead to a harness and the second to a wide fitting collar—something like a whippet collar or fish-tail collar (see *pic*) is helpful as it spreads the load on the neck area—so your trainee can be comfortable wearing his familiar harness and also be controlled more easily using the lead attached to his collar. Having two leads can be 'a bit of a fiddle' when walking, so some people opt for a single lead with a clip at each end. Using a 'double-ended clip lead' (see *pic*) you can attach one end of this lead to the collar and clip the other end to the harness. This system can work well as a schooling aid.

The message here is that harnesses certainly present great value in different situations but if you are using one to walk your dog and he's pulling you like a train and you have little control, then you may need to rethink your strategy and change your toolset.

Head gear

A head collar and a figure-of-8 lead are a couple of the most popular lead-walking accessories. These tools have been developed from observations of how horses, livestock and other large animals can be easily led using a lead and head collar. We know that if we use this tool effectively, we can guide the head in a particular direction and the rest of the body will follow. Head collars, figure-of-8 leads and others apply the same concept of 'leading' to our canines. These are very useful tools, particularly when controlling dogs prone to intense pulling on-lead behaviour.

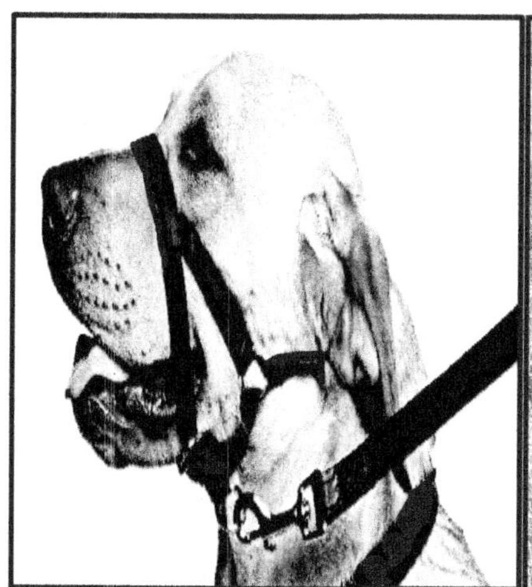

Haltee Head Collar

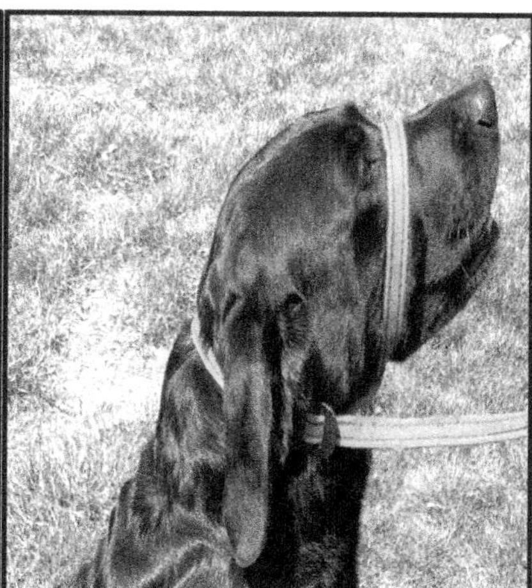

Figure-of-8 Lead

The size of head collar is very important. If it's too big, it will be uncomfortable and will probably move into or over your dog's eyes and he may wriggle out of it. If it's too small, it can pinch a dog's muzzle and eyes and prove uncomfortably tight, so check the manufacturer's guidelines to ensure you select the correct size for your trainee. Many pet shops actively welcome you to try products on your dog when you visit them in store, so take this route if you decide to investigate a tool like this. Some good online shops will ask you to measure parts of your dog's head and muzzle and enter these figures into a program to find the best size/fit for your dog.

A figure of 8 lead is a 'one size fits all' lead (so no measuring is required) but they do come in different thicknesses and some are padded etc., so you will need to do a little research here and find one that suits your trainee.

If you have a very exuberant trainee at home and don't have enough strength or control to even begin to practice 'walking nicely,' then using a head collar or similar accessory is worth considering. If you do decide to try one, please invest time—a few days—getting your trainee used to the new item 'on his face.' He needs to feel comfortable with it before you use it outside on a walk, so spend some time in the lounge or garden playing with your trainee and, during these games, put the new item on for very short time periods and lead him from A to B around the home—use treats and toys during the new experience so he gets used to the idea.

Exercise first, then train

Think about practising some brief training routines like 'Sit, Stay, Come, Fetch' for ten minutes or so to help drain your trainee's energy levels a little *before* you walk, which can be very valuable. If he really loves cheese or a tug toy, then use these when interacting with and stimulating him. Your goal here is not to get your trainee into a heightened or amber state at all, but to engage with him positively while achieving a reasonable level of responsiveness at home (through play) just ahead of 'walking time.'

Select your training environment carefully

If you have a dog who is a 'real puller' on-lead, then it stands to reason that you should practice walking in a quiet area initially so you can cultivate good walking skills. Don't head off to the park where lots of distractions—people and other dogs—will be present, as this will probably prove too stimulating for your trainee and end up only sabotaging your training efforts. Build up positive experiences at first by walking around a quiet village or in a remote part of town and, once you are seeing improvements, you can then think about walking in a more challenging environment. Make a mental note of a few suitable venues you could visit daily and consider when you will walk too—avoid busy times.

Choose a side

Once you've thought about where you might practice lead walking in the early phases of training, you'll need to decide where you want your trainee, Trixie, to be when walking alongside you—on the left or on the right side—and ask everyone at home to stick to walking her on the same side so this is completely consistent, at least in the very early stages of training. The usual approach is to walk Trixie on your left side but if you have a good reason or just a preference for the right, then walk her there. It's very important that you feel comfortable when walking your trainee, so choose the side that suits you best. When walking, create a mental picture of a virtual hula-hoop of space on your left or right side—your goal is to school Trixie so she knows to remain inside this virtual hoop (alongside you) whenever you say "Heel" or "Close" as you both move forward on a walk.

Holding your lead correctly

So, assuming you have identified a suitable walking tool/accessory—many will choose a simple lead and collar—and have decided what side Trixie will walk on, start by placing a lead on her and position her directly alongside you, either sitting or standing (see *pic 1*).

Once she's beside you, slide your hand (the one nearest Trixie) down the lead until it meets her collar or neck (see *pic 2*). Then slowly slide it back up the lead again until you reach your hip area (see *pic 3*). This is where the hand (nearest the dog) needs to be on the lead—and where it needs to remain—when you walk. You could call this your 'dog hand,' the one that 'listens' to your dog when walking. Keeping your 'dog hand' in this position, now focus on relaxing your arm and lead a little so it's smiling (see *pic 4)*.

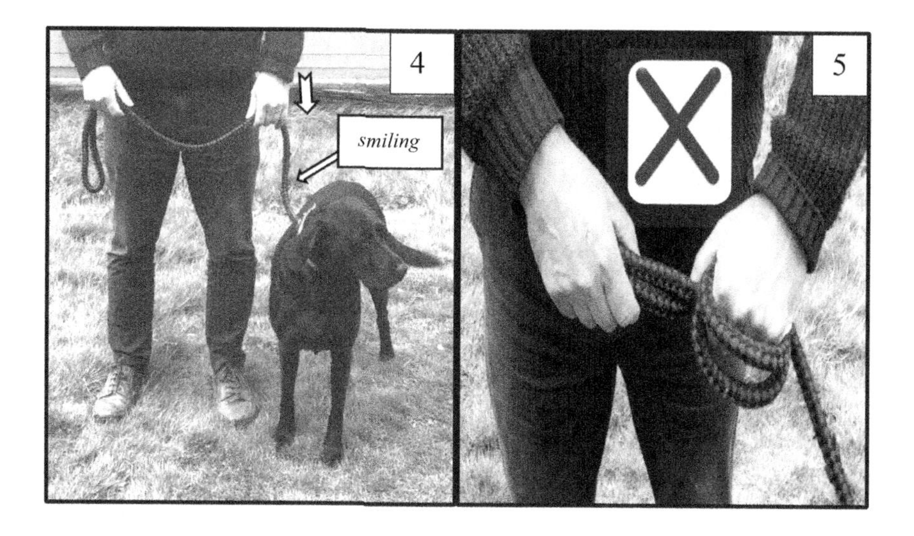

It's important to keep the palm of your 'dog hand' facing the ground (see *pic 4)* as you maintain a smiling lead—try to get out of the habit of ever turning your palm upwards. Also, always avoid wrapping the lead around your hand (see *pic 5*)—take hold of your lead using a green vibe, keeping your 'dog hand' relaxed (see *pic 4)* rather than grabbing the lead and holding it in any kind of tense manner. Please note that your 'dog hand' should not be holding any treats, poo bags or your phone etc. so you'll be able to focus on how your trainee 'feels' and really connect on a walk … and vice versa. The other hand can take up any slack in the lead.

Lures

Once you have a clear picture in your mind about what 'good walking practice' looks like (i.e., how you will hold the lead, which side your trainee is going to walk, where you will train), you're ready to start practising. You could start by holding a lure/enticement … maybe a favourite ball, toy

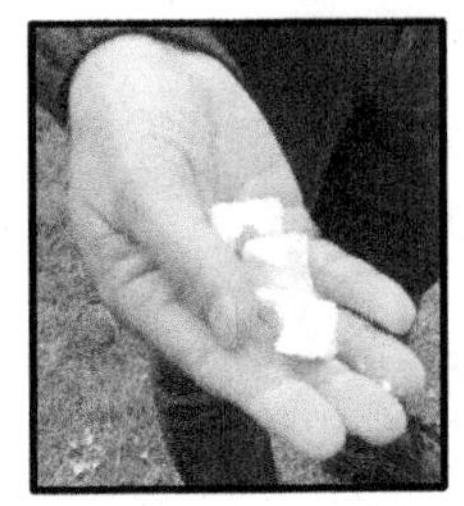

or high value food reward (cooked chicken, liver cake, cheese) while saying "Close" as this will motivate your trainee to get into the correct position more readily, given that Trixie will be very intent on looking at or checking out the interesting lure. You'll have to move the lure hand around a little at first to see what lure position works best for you when trying to keep Trixie in the correct 'Close' position. But after a little trial and error, you'll find the best place to hold the lure in order to keep Trixie alongside and focused on you. Once she's remained in the correct walking position for a short time, give the reward and remember to say "Gooood Close" to reinforce the positive behaviour.

Any time she moves out of the correct position beside you, disagree with this behaviour, remembering to say "Ah-Ah" followed quickly by "Trixie, Wait" if you need to regain a little control. Then indicate that you want her to get into the correct position by giving your "Trixie, Close" verbal command (while showing her the lure) just before you move. Whenever Trixie gets into the correct position alongside and your lead is smiling, remember to verbally give some up-beat praise ("Gooood Close") just at the right time—as she moves effortlessly on a walk with you. Trixie will soon get the idea that 'Close' means 'walk alongside.'

Introduce a 'Touch' command

It can be useful to condition a 'Touch' behaviour too to get Trixie to come right into you and touch your hand with her nose as you walk along together. A good idea is to start practising the 'Touch' game at home before using it on a walk. Start by using a few treats and invite Trixie to come to you, saying "Touch" a couple of times just as you take a step back from her. She will follow you … and the tasty treats or toy. Then say "Touch" again in a welcoming manner, trying to get her to make light contact with your hand (holding the treat/toy). Once her muzzle or nose touches your hand, immediately give a treat or toy and inject *lots* of verbal praise: "Gooood Touch." Later in the day, practice again with a favourite toy, using an excited verbal, "Trixie, Come" and "Trixie, Touch." If she comes to you and makes light contact with her nose/muzzle, quickly offer the toy and play a game. Before long Trixie will learn that 'Touch' means 'move in and make contact with the hand' ... and good things follow.

When walking together outside, whenever Trixie moves a little too far forward alongside you on a walk, you can say "Touch" to bring her back into the correct position—within your virtual hula-hoop—and follow this with praise and a 'Close' command before continuing on your walk. By conditioning a good 'Touch' behaviour like this you will have a useful control tool when out walking with your trainee. You might also like to try some of the following exercises too—these will challenge your trainee and will certainly improve the 'Close' behaviour, as well as giving you a better idea of any area that needs a little work. If you are upbeat and green when teaching, most dogs really love these 'walking games,' so try them yourself at home and in the park.

Weaving

The 'weaving game' is a great one to practice. Simply place four or five markers on the ground, arranged about one or two metres apart in a straight line—you can place some

cones or canes down in your garden or local park, for example. Begin by walking around the outside of the cones with your on-lead trainee, going down one side and then up the other. After a short time reward your trainee and start using your "Close" command before weaving in and out of the cones. Use your lure wisely, trying to keep your trainee focused on you as you walk. Stop after a few circuits of weaving in and out through the cones and reward heartily. After a short break, restart your weaving again and finish training by engaging in an off-lead game with a ball or favourite toy. You can arrange the markers in a square or circle formation as well, so do give this a go too. Vary your routines every day and remember to always add 'high value' praise whenever you get the responses you are looking for.

Figure of 8

You might also like to try the 'figure of 8' routine. Place two markers or cones on the ground about two metres apart. The idea is that you start at one end, walking around one cone in a clockwise manner before cutting between both cones and walking in an anti-clockwise direction around the other. Then walk back again, cutting in through the cones to complete a figure of 8. Continue making your 'figures of 8' and try moving in the opposite direction too at times. This will condition your dog to take up a very good 'Close' position no matter what direction you move in, so it's definitely worth practising if you want to have a really well-schooled trainee.

More than one command

Building up combinations of commands like 'Close,' 'Touch,' 'Wait,' 'Sit', 'Fetch' is a great idea and should be great fun for both trainer and trainee. Always finish by rewarding responsiveness—this might involve throwing a toy/ball excitedly or playing 'find' with some treats which will really help reinforce positive behaviour.

Practice makes perfect, so use enticing lures along with a confident and positive attitude—cultivated from having a clear strategy in mind—and you should have your trainee walking nicely alongside you quite quickly. Once you feel fairly confident with the on-lead 'Close' command, you can then start practising the 'Close' behaviour when off-lead as well. If you're having persistent 'pulling-on-lead' issues, consider joining a good dog training group or get some one-to-one professional advice from a trainer/behaviourist, so you can ask questions and get some practical support.

MANNERS

Chapter 13

Respect

Growing up in Ireland with my two brothers, we'd often eat our main meal together in the evening around 6pm. As a young lad, if I was playing outside (usually with a dog or a ball ... or both) and one of my brothers came to the door to shout, "Brian, come inside—your dinner's ready!" I'd probably shout back saying, "Okay!" ... but generally, I didn't budge. Often, the call would come again—and maybe again—before I'd finally make a move. On the other hand, if my father or mother came to the door, all they had to say was "Brian" in a tone that meant 'Come in now' and I would move indoors straight away. The point here is that the request I was getting from both parties was the same, but my reactions were very different.

My parents had my respect, cultivated from years of acknowledging and praising my behaviour when it was good and also saying, "I don't think so" to any misbehaviour, so I had already been conditioned to listen and respond quickly to them. My brothers, my peers, had to work much harder to get positive feedback as they didn't have quite enough standing or respect in my mind to suggest 'what I should do,' so I was often less responsive to their requests. Obviously, respect is very important when considering the human-human connection and it's much the same when we examine human-canine interactions.

Gaining a little more respect simply involves playing your positive teacher role that we mentioned earlier. You (definitely) don't have to turn into a 'Sergeant Major' or become a different person at all—it just means that you should invest some time teaching your dog to know what's expected by guiding him positively ... praising at key times and disagreeing with misbehaviour (in a very reasonable manner) at others. Dogs love this consistent approach and crave a clear understanding of how things work, being shown what is welcome and unwelcome behaviour.

Of course, if you have a trainee that's already very balanced and fairly easy going, one who gets on very well with other dogs and people in varied situations and he listens to you consistently when asked to "Come," for example, then respect and responsivity are already in place. There's no need to do anything differently—a great relationship already exists; well done you, keep doing what you're doing. However, if you have a trainee that tunes you out whenever it suits him and behaves like a mini-hooligan at times, then teaching him some manners—showing him 'how to behave well' at different times—will prove very useful, if harmony and increased responsiveness are what you're looking for at home and when you're out and about together.

So, if having a reasonable level of respect is very important to our teaching role and improving responsiveness, what opportunities can we grab hold of to convince our trainees to listen more to our direction? If we think about the phrase 'manners show respect,' what manners should we teach our trainees?

In the next few chapters, we'll explore strategies that will answer these questions. Our goal here is to build confidence and cultivate responsiveness in our trainees—young or old—while fostering mutual understanding.

Chapter 14

Behaviour at Home

Leaving home together

Most dogs are naturally going to get a little worked up when you decide to go out for a dog walk ... a super exciting time! So, let's explore what 'starting your walk' might look like and focus on teaching a few manners in the early stages—particularly important if you have a trainee who gets really over-the-top when starting out on a walk. If you have a clear strategy in mind then it will be much easier to teach your trainee how you want the story to unfold.

When leaving home, try to make a point of calling your dog to you first (even if he's right beside you) and ask him to 'Sit' and 'Wait' in front of you while you put on his lead. It's important to make the statement of calling him to you at the initial stage so the pattern of going for a walk begins with responsiveness on his part. Once your trainee has come to you and is sitting, reward him quietly by saying "Good boy" and "Good Sit" as you put his lead on.

As outlined earlier when mentioning the dangers of 'nurturing the wrong colour,' if your trainee's already right next to you getting really excited and jumping around at the sight of the lead, just stop and consider what message you're giving here. If you put the lead on when your dog is clearly wearing a high amber mind then you're saying you regard this as favourable behaviour—offering great value for behaving in an over-the-top manner. Only put his lead on if your trainee's behaving (fairly) respectfully; otherwise, wait until he stops jumping around and becomes more reasonable—showing a low amber or, if you can get it, a green mind. A little excitement is completely fine, but we do need to ask for some manners here. Avoid talking too much to your trainee at this stage and disagree immediately with any excitement by asking him to "Wait" or "Sit" immediately if you need to. The message you are intent on communicating is: 'If you listen to me and behave well at key times, we can move forward; otherwise, we'll just wait.' As soon as you see that your trainee is waiting fairly patiently, say "Good boy" and pop his lead on, open the door and ask him to "Wait" again with you inside the doorway for about ten seconds or so. Once you've achieved this step successfully, you're ready to start leaving the home to go for a walk. When thinking about this strategy, you could pretend you have been given the task of training an assistance dog, your dog—this concept might prove very motivating for some.

As a good teacher, you really shouldn't practice letting your dog pull you forward through the doorway while making the lead taut, or he'll learn that he can accelerate the walk by not really having any regard for the person being towed behind. Manners please! Some trainers focus on the dog's position relative to the handler here, being quite rigid about the fact that a trainee should never be in front of you when exiting the home. However, we should focus more on the cues we are giving and what's happening with the lead in this situation. If your dog waits for your cue to move out of the home—you could say "Okay" or "Close," for example, to signal that 'We're done waiting, let's go'—and, provided his colour is reasonable and the lead doesn't get taut, even if your trainee is ahead of you, then leave the home and start the walk. Your trainee was listening to you and followed your cues, so he was behaving very well, even if he moved in front of you as you left the home. We're looking for a reasonable 'leaving the home' routine and a little more respect and manners here, that's all. Remember to stay green and, whenever the lead becomes taut or his colour becomes too high, simply say "Ah-Ah, Wait" quickly before calmly repositioning your trainee inside the home to restart the exercise.

Asking your dog to remain respectful while leaving the home might appear an almost insignificant detail to us, but it can be quite significant in your dog's mind. Try it. Develop a basic routine to apply every time you set out on a walk and mentally rehearse how you really want to begin the walk at home. Do you have a strategy that you use daily? What does the beginning of your walk look like ... you get the lead and then what happens? Specifically, what could you change about your vibe and approach? Does everyone at home use the same system?

Returning home with your trainee

Returning home after a walk with your trainee provides another opportunity to practice a few manners. Before entering the home, ask him to "Wait" and/or "Sit" at the front door for a very short time. Praise him using "Good boy, good Wait" when he completes the brief waiting exercise and then offer your verbal cue ("Okay" or "In") and maybe offer a visual cue—a simple pointing gesture—to signal 'let's move indoors.' Here, you're developing a positive system your trainee can easily understand—your underlying message is to offer clear direction consistently and convey the message, 'Manners please!'

If you use a positive vibe and reward regularly, your trainee will wait automatically as he approaches your front door, provided that everyone at home is consistent. Life for your trainee will be much simpler too, as he will have learnt what's expected (manners) and will listen to you far more, both indoors and outside, as a result of simple routines.

When you return home to your dog

If you've been to work, gone shopping or were visiting Aunty Anne and left your dog Zena at home, when you return and are about to put your key in the front door, think about 'colours' and how you will behave as you enter the home. Good teachers will try to get into the habit of nurturing positive (green or low amber) minds and playing down (i.e., giving little value to) any negative colours.

If your trainee is going berserk with excitement, then adding to the chaos by saying, "Hello, baby Zena … I'm back! Yipeeee! … I missed you!! Gooood girl!!" in a heightened way is probably not a great starting point, as you are promoting this exuberant behaviour and colour and not really acting like a great teacher—and definitely not asking for any manners. Try to avoid saying other things too, like, "Get off, Zena … stop jumping, Zena … No! … get down …

silly girl … you are SO naughty!" as this human behaviour will only excite and add value, and your trainee's colour is likely to get worse over time. Association.

Instead, if Zena is super-excited on your return, consider reducing your level of interaction by pretending your trainee isn't there at all for about thirty seconds or so and, after a very short time, call Zena to you and make your greetings then, having waited for her colour to settle a little. Try to distract yourself from what's happening with your trainee in the beginning by greeting any adults or children at home first, putting some water in the kettle quickly or by just looking out of the window for a few moments. Do your best not to look at or interact with an over-excited Zena but, after a very short time has passed, call her over—if she's not there already—and make a great fuss of her. You are making the subtle but key statement that you acknowledge and reward good manners and good colours, but don't welcome any overt excitement when you return home. If you return home and Zena comes to you with a slightly excited (but reasonable) colour, then feel free to acknowledge this approach and mindset by praising/interacting sooner than the thirty second guideline.

Some owners shy away from even trying this technique, worried their dog's feelings will be hurt or that their trainee might even feel rejected in some way. Remember, you're still going to give your trainee all that love, affection and attention, it's just delayed for a very short time. Your goal is to teach Zena some manners and etiquette, that's all. If all family members sing from the same hymn sheet and are as consistent as possible when returning home, great rewards will be reaped.

Ask friends or visitors to behave!

While not always practical, try to involve people visiting the home in the new 'visiting and greeting' regime too—family members, friends and neighbours are often happy to help. Once visitors have been in the home for a very short time and have done their best to ignore Zena, assuming your trainee is wearing a green or low amber mind, ask them to call her over and give her some affection, once you've decided the time for introductions is right. This will help set the tone for when the next visitor arrives at your home. If, of course, Zena approaches visitors at home with a green or low amber mind very early on, ask your guests to acknowledge this colour and to give her quiet affection, to promote this behaviour for the future and send the clear message that, 'yes, this is what we like to see.'

So, in summary … try to pay attention to how you enter your home to greet your trainee and also take more notice of his behaviour and colour as he enters and leaves the home with you. Stay green and guide him … 'manners please' is your core message. Also, show your trainee how to behave when people visit you at home by developing a clear routine he can easily follow—use your lead indoors too at times if you feel this will help, always remembering to nurture positive colours and behaviour.

Chapter 15

Dog Yoga

Most of us love seeing our dogs flying after a ball or favourite toy in the garden or doing some 'zoomies' with other dogs in the park and, while these energetic interactions are very positive and useful, we should 'balance things out' and spend some time practising being quiet and steady with our trainees too. When we spoke about using your lead as a 'control tool' earlier, we highlighted the idea of putting your dog on a lead indoors and asking him to settle alongside you while, for example, you have a cup of tea at various times during the day. This 'Dog Yoga' routine is a *very* useful exercise you could practice at home on a regular basis, particularly if you have a trainee who spends a lot of time stuck in an amber mind throughout the day. 'Dog Yoga' doesn't look or feel like you're doing very much, but it presents great value for both teacher and trainee, where both practice 'waiting patiently' together with green minds.

<u>How to practice</u>

During a quiet time in the day when there's not too much happening at home, simply call your trainee to you and put on his lead. If he's going to get too excited when you bring out his usual (walking) lead then buy or borrow a different one—you could call this your indoor 'Yoga lead?' Place the lead on your trainee and position him so that he's next to you, on one side or the other, as you sit down on a chair or sofa—your trainee should be on the floor. Think of it as having a virtual hula hoop of space to the right and left of you ... start by guiding your trainee into one of these 'hoops'. Your goal should be that he stays within his hoop in a waiting state until you decide to finish the exercise. Don't ask him to 'Stay' or anything else at all; just say "Settle"—meaning 'relax alongside me.' Your trainee can, of course, stand, sit or lay down and move around during the exercise too—but he should not move too far out of his original hoop/space or make the lead taut, and he must remain on the floor and on-lead throughout. If he moves too far out of place and creates tension in the lead, then say "No" or "Ah-Ah" and maybe stand up and calmly reposition him if you need to, again giving the 'Settle' cue word just before you sit down and start again. Using a word like 'Settle' or 'Relax' to cue your trainee is useful here as, over time, this word will be associated with achieving a green and waiting mindset which you can then use effectively in different situations. Positive verbal feedback ('Gooood Settle!'), lots of cuddles and head massages can and should be given at times throughout Yoga (quietly, of course), provided your trainee is wearing a green or low amber mind. Remain positive, persistent and green.

Practice is important, as it might take a few trial runs for your trainee to get the 'settling' idea. Maybe place his bed beside you initially so he has somewhere to settle comfortably alongside; this might help him understand that this is a waiting and relaxing exercise and he is very likely to calm down more quickly and stay green for longer as a result.

When to practice

Introduce the 'Dog Yoga' exercise soon after you've returned from a walk or after playing a game, when your trainee will naturally be more inclined to rest. You should practice in five-minute sessions initially and then gradually extend this to fifteen or twenty-minutes. You don't need to do this every day, but try to do it at least a few times a week so your trainee gets really good at waiting with you.

So, the next time you make a cup of tea or coffee, consider doing some 'Dog Yoga' with your trainee! Simply call him to you, put his indoor lead on, move to where you will be sitting, ask him to "Settle" and enjoy your break. As mentioned already, do make a quiet fuss of him when he's settled, by stroking his head or ears in a soothing manner and tell him how wonderful he is by saying "Good Settle" now and again. If you are giving cuddles and petting to a green or low amber mind, that's great; otherwise, stop sharing affection—it's not the right time or colour. Once you've completed your exercise, take the lead off your trainee and calmly say, "Good boy" and "Good Settle."

When to use 'Dog Yoga'

You can use your 'Dog Yoga' routine when visitors arrive at home, when children or elderly people are present, when you visit a pub or café with your dog or when you just want to practice something peaceful with your trainee indoors. Once you've conditioned the behaviour you can also use your 'Settle' command whenever your trainee is moving into a negative colour. If he's getting too excited around other dogs or children or if he's pacing in the car or getting uptight in your vet's waiting room, for example, this command will prove really useful.

Please avoid using 'Yoga' as any kind of punitive measure where, for example, one day you're really fed up with Samson because he's chewed up your favourite shoes and you can be heard ranting in the bedroom, "Right, that's it, Samson, I've had enough of all this ... *you* can do 'Dog Yoga' for half an hour because of your horrible behaviour!" This is not what 'Dog Yoga' is about (and clearly you have already left the green zone!)—instead, focus on practising very positive 15-minute waiting sessions during the week.

What has 'Dog Yoga' got to do with manners?

If we imagine looking at a video clip of you practising your 'Dog Yoga' at home, we would see that you're sitting down with your on-lead trainee waiting alongside, hopefully in a settled state of mind. He's waiting for you—his teacher—to signal what will happen next ... maybe you will give him more cuddles or take his lead off or invite him onto the sofa with you or move from the lounge to the kitchen or stay put for a while longer? A key point to note is that he's relaxing and having a lovely time during the 'Settle' exercise—getting a head and body massage or cuddles too at times—so he will get better at wearing a patient and green mind indoors. A stronger bond and increased levels of respect will follow if teacher and trainee practice waiting and 'being green together' regularly.

Chapter 16

Using Food Wisely

What and how to feed

Most of us appreciate the effect our own diet has on our physical and mental well-being and this is also true when we hone in on our trainee's eating habits. If you want a balanced canine mind at home then it makes sense to nurture this by selecting *quality food* for your trainee.

Dogs need enough of the 'right nutrients' if they are to remain healthy: water, proteins, fats, vitamins and minerals (Note: research has shown that dogs don't need carbohydrates to thrive—they get all they need from the other five nutrients). As well as making sure our dogs are getting enough appropriate nutrition every day, we should do our very best to avoid any 'fillers', preservatives, additives or colourings in their food or treats.

When it comes to answering the question: 'What is the best food to choose for my dog?' there really is a *vast* amount of choice and there are *many* different opinions on the matter. Let's start by looking into the different ways of feeding—outlined below—and then it would be a great idea to do some additional research before you decide what's really best for your dog. This is his mental and physical wellbeing we're considering, so any investigating on your part is time *very* well spent.

Food for thought

1) 'Kibble' food

- ☺ Kibble is also referred to as 'dog biscuits' or 'dry food' and is an economical way of feeding.
- ☺ The range includes ingredients like beef, chicken, turkey, lamb and fish varieties (among others).
- ☺ Kibble is easily available in supermarkets and pet shops and comes in bags/sacks of various sizes.
- ☺ It is simple to store, has a very long shelf life and is easily measured out into appropriate feeding quantities.

- ☹ While feeding kibble is very convenient and familiar—many of us have grown up feeding family dogs like this—it often has a very high carbohydrate content which is not appropriate for dogs/carnivores.
- ☹ Kibble is produced by cooking ingredients for long periods (often at *very* high temperatures) so the nutritional value of the end-product should certainly be investigated.
- ☹ Kibble is usually a single protein feed—your dog might eat the same 'turkey and rice' option every day for months at a time—which is much too restrictive in terms of protein consumption. Dogs should have variety here.

- ☹ Some research suggests that a dog's gut health, overall wellbeing and life-span/longevity could be negatively affected if fed like this over time.

2) 'Tinned' or 'Canned' food

- ☺ Tinned dog food is, of course, very convenient—just open the can, scoop it into your dog's bowl ... job done.
- ☺ Contents are varied and often include chicken or beef, turkey, fish etc. and some products have vegetables, pasta and other ingredients, all bound together in a (solid) loaf form or in a 'jelly' or 'gravy'.
- ☺ Like kibble, grain-free and wheat-free options are available in tinned varieties.

- ☹ If the bulk of your feeding regime will comprise tinned food, you will need to check your labels very carefully. Examine product details in more depth online too to see if the ingredients are of good quality and free from additives, preservatives and other nasties—try to ensure the overall composition is appropriate for your dog.
- ☹ The tinned food you select should be minimally processed and must have enough nutritional value to fulfil your trainee. You may need to add ingredients and variety here to ensure you are providing a balanced diet.

3) 'Wet,' 'Moist,' or 'Pouch' food

- ☺ This type of dog food is easily available and is very convenient to store and use.
- ☺ It can often prove very appealing to some (often smaller) dogs who might not be too keen on crunching kibble or eating tinned food.

- 😮 While many small dogs are fed this way, products can contain a large percentage of water making it more expensive per calorie than kibble or tinned.
- 😮 It might also have quite high levels of sugar and salt, so it's important to check labels very carefully to see if this food can provide a balanced diet for your dog ... or maybe you'll need to include other key ingredients to boost your dog's daily nutrition.

4) 'Home-cooked' food

- ☺ Some owners feed their dogs home-cooked chicken, turkey, lamb, beef, pork or fish and add a little cooked rice or pasta or vegetables too at times. Raw or cooked eggs are often given a couple of times a week as an added extra. Many dogs will enjoy the variety (in terms of taste) that home-cooked meals provide.

- ☹ We should be very aware that our goal is to feed a balanced *canine diet* and not one that is nutritionally appropriate for humans. We should adopt an approach to feeding that is 'species specific.'
- ☹ This method of feeding can be very time consuming and quite an expensive process for an owner, particularly if you have more than one large dog at home.

5) 'Raw' food

- ☺ Owners who are not keen on feeding kibble, tinned or wet food often choose to 'feed raw', which can present noticeable positive differences in physical and mental wellbeing by boosting a dog's gut health due to the increased levels of valuable nutrients and enzymes present in raw (uncooked) ingredients.
- ☺ Meats/proteins can easily be varied throughout the week which is excellent news for your trainee.
- ☺ Owners can choose to buy individual ready-to-serve 'Complete' raw feeding packs or make up their own recipes by combining specific amounts of raw meat, offal and bone—some like to add a few vegetables too.

- ☹ While raw feeding only involves storing and defrosting pre-prepared packs of raw food, for most of us, shifting from a familiar feeding regime to a new one can seem quite daunting at first.
- ☹ Anyone thinking about feeding raw will need to do some research to find out how to do this correctly.
- ☹ You will need to have enough freezer space to store the frozen food, which might be a consideration if you have more than one medium/large dog.
- ☹ If you have a few large dogs at home then purchasing packs of frozen raw food may become costly.

On a personal note, having fed my own dogs a variety of kibble and tinned foods for over forty years, my preference and recommendation now is to feed raw (uncooked) ingredients sourced from a reputable raw food supplier, often with a little additional support from a local butcher. While I'm convinced that feeding a varied raw diet is the best feeding method for so many reasons, it falls to each of us to complete our own research and then decide on the best way forward. Think about joining some dog feeding groups online and consider getting in touch with a reputable animal nutritionist. Also, start chatting with people in your area who have dogs that are physically and mentally in top form so you can explore and maybe mimic what and how they feed. Focus on feeding *quality* … use food that will provide the maximum nutritional benefit for your dog.

Treats

Some shop-bought treats can be very tasty and your dog is likely to have his favourites; however, some products have ingredients that might negatively affect your dog's tummy and behaviour so it's important to check things out—veer towards natural ingredients and (far) away from any preservatives, additives or colourings. Think about searching online for 'air-dried and freeze-dried dog treats' … the results should offer some healthy options. Also, experiment a little at home—consider making your own liver cake or cheesy treats *(two recipes you might try are available at the end of this section*) or reward using cooked chicken/bacon bits or some raw carrot sticks. There are lots of DIY dog treat recipes available online that take very little time or effort to prepare, are really tasty and quite healthy for your dog. So, after doing a little research, hopefully you'll feel creative and might get cooking! A good idea is to cook/bake quite a lot in one go and freeze most of the treats using small freezer bags that you can take out and defrost at will. Your trainee will love these healthy rewards … and green minds should stay green.

Standard or high-value food rewards

Your trainee is very likely to respond very well to the practice of getting standard food treats for good behaviour and high-value treats for fabulous performance. The thinking here is in sync with the notion of praising a dog by using a 'medium and high' system of verbal feedback, outlined earlier. Some of your dog's kibble or treats bought from a pet shop will fall into the 'standard treat' category, whereas an 'excellent treat' might be a few small pieces of cheddar cheese, cooked chicken or some liver-cake. Some well-intentioned owners give lots of high-value treats to a trainee that is doing something 'ordinary'—something like the 'Sit' behaviour that he's been practising for years—but this isn't really the best way to motivate. A good teacher will want to make a distinction in the trainee's mind between 'good' and 'excellent' behaviour and will match the level of reward to what has been achieved. If your trainee's just been playing with other dogs in the park and—once he hears your recall or 'Come' command—chooses to run enthusiastically in your direction then the 'excellent' or high-value treats are definitely the ones to reach for.

Take a little time to think about what behaviours merit high-value treats—the recall or 'Come' command is definitely one of these. What other behaviours would you really like to perfect? Maybe you could give your trainee a super-high-value treat if he's behaving extremely well when visitors arrive. It would be great if you could pass a few high-value treats to your visitors too, so they can promote good behaviour if they see a green or low-amber canine mind welcoming them (provided this won't over stimulate your trainee.)

How to treat

As outlined already, when your trainee responds correctly to the 'Sit,' for example, he might get a tasty food treat as soon as his bottom touches the floor. While this practice is great when training any new behaviour, we must try (hard) to avoid over-treating. If we give a food treat for everything our dog does, it makes sense that he'll come to expect this human behaviour over time. Then, if a treat isn't presented, your trainee is likely to get confused … 'why didn't I get anything nice that time?' So, quite early on, as your dog's training progresses, try to shift your focus away from giving food rewards every single time to a system that motivates by giving a food treat only after a series of instructions have been carried out together—like a 'Sit,' 'Stay,' 'Come' routine—progressively asking 'more for less.' As training moves ahead even more, you could begin to gradually phase treats out completely so your trainee doesn't become expectant on food rewards and, when they appear at key times in the future, they will be very well received!

Positive verbal feedback, hearty petting, excited hand clapping, a ball, a frisbee, a squeaky toy, an animated teacher, a game or a walk are all great substitutes for food treats and serve as great rewards. Show your trainee that you're delighted with him in varied ways—this approach will strengthen your bond and promote good behaviour for the future.

Taking food up

Some owners aren't too bothered if their dog takes all day to eat his meal and are happy to leave food down all the time. Their dog, if used to this system, might eat a little and then move away, usually returning later on to have a little bit more and so it goes throughout the day. At different times, a member of the household or maybe everyone at home, seeing the contents of the food bowl getting low, might go into top-up or refill mode. Feeding like this can encourage a trainee to become very selective and often a picky eater, given they learn quickly that food is available all the time. They might also figure out that if they only eat a little, an alternative menu or some special treats will be served up because very kind owners try to compensate.

Aside from any health and digestive issues that could arise when feeding in this way, we're really promoting unnatural canine behaviour here. Dogs aren't naturally conditioned to having a restaurant-on-tap type of lifestyle and, like us, also benefit from having time to digest their food and experience occasional periods when food isn't readily available. If there's more than one dog in the home, competition usually motivates all of them to eat what's in front of them while it's in front of them—otherwise, they learn that they risk coming back to nothing. This keenness for food is something we should expect in any healthy dog rather than becoming used to seeing them eat a little now and again, whenever they want.

A more natural system to adopt around feeding time is to place your dog's food bowl down and make a mental note to take it up again after five minutes or so, whether the food has been eaten or not. If it hasn't been eaten within a reasonable time take it up and serve it again later in the day, provided it's still in good order of course. By applying the same strategy every day, the new system will be understood quickly. Simply dispose of food that isn't eaten by the second meal, particularly if it's not kibble/dry food, and start afresh the following day. Soon your trainee will learn that abandoning food means that another serving will not be coming along for a while, so eating everything in one sitting should become automatic—a much more natural and healthier option for your trainee.

Obviously, it makes sense to do your research and find a food that is healthy and one he really likes—then stick with this for a time at least, to develop the routine of eating 'there and then.' Motivate him to want to eat by mixing a few tasty treats in with his food or smearing a little fish oil (or something else he loves) at the bottom of his bowl, if you think this will get him to eat more keenly. This new manner of regular feeding will also allow you to understand and monitor your trainee's daily intake of food more accurately, which is really valuable if you're trying to build him up or manage his calorie intake. A system where an adult dog eats a couple of times a day, for example, alongside durations of time when food is not being consumed, will support your dog's digestive system and this routine will greatly improve his toilet behaviour too. Significantly, you'll get some 'bonus points' here as well, earnt from the perspective where your trainee sees you as the one who always provides great value … his next meal.

Bribery

Otto, your Uncle Tom's rescue dog, is 'a bit of a handful' and occasionally decides he's not going to sit down for your uncle when asked. This always proves embarrassing for Tom whenever you visit. Tom, after bellowing a few sharp "Sittt" instructions in Otto's direction, starts to feel frustrated and slightly embarrassed—particularly as family and friends look on—so an urgent 'plan B' is thought up and a juicy food treat is offered. Hey-presto, Otto gets the message and sits down straight away and is given a few lovely treats along with some verbal and physical praise. As I'm sure you appreciate, Otto didn't listen to his teacher for a time and only decided he'd cooperate when treats were on offer—then Tom rewarded him heartily ... not really a great teaching strategy to follow. In a situation like this, putting a lead on Otto and then calmly asking him to "Sit" again is one good approach, rather than involving treats at all. When he does 'Sit' some verbal and physical praise are appropriate here. Later on, when Otto offers the 'Sit' behaviour straight away, definitely reward this kind of response with exuberant verbal and physical praise alongside a tasty food treat.

Any good dog owner will strive for a bond well beyond a canine mind that will only listen when a juicy treat is on offer, so please be careful not to start any bad habits that you might have to undo later on. Be a clear teacher. Definitely *do* use food to reward and certainly motivate your trainee like this at key times but avoid using tasty treats as any kind of bargaining tool.

Begging at the table

Some people might be completely fine about their sweet natured Nico approaching them while they are eating. Some may offer food when this happens too—often feeling guilty about eating when Nico looks at them 'in that way.' Please recognise that if you promote this begging behaviour (by giving value) then you have to be okay about it *all* of the time ... it would be very unfair to give Nico a nice treat sometimes and to tell him off at others. If you only give your trainee a titbit from the table or drop an occasional morsel on the floor once in a very blue moon, you're driving the expectation in his mind that there could be value/rewards at some point in the future around your mealtime. Everyone at home must agree to a clear strategy here—most of us will opt for the sensible 'No treating from the table' or 'No treating while humans eat' system—and there should be no exceptions, as these will only slow down the process of conditioning good behaviour (manners) in your trainee.

Simply take Nico to where you want him to be while you eat (which might be right beside you or in his bed a little way from you) and ask him to 'Settle' and 'Stay' while you enjoy your peaceful meal. Please be patient and don't fall into that guilt trap that Nico's soppy canine eyes will probably lay on you. If you need to ask Nico to return to his bed a few times and to 'Stay', then so be it. Remember … Nico's still going to get the titbits, but just a little later, at a time that will promote good manners.

Also, if you're already fairly used to leaving the table after a meal and, while clearing away plates and any leftovers, think to yourself: 'I'll just give these few bits and pieces to Nico now,' then you might consider breaking some old habits! Of course, it feels great to give food to Nico and see him enjoying it, but this isn't the right time. If you give Nico some food even occasionally when returning to the kitchen, you're conditioning yet another begging behaviour—one that will cause him to look forward to the sound of knives and forks clearing plates, signifying the end of the meal and his long-awaited reward. Some dogs will whine and can easily start drooling near the end of a human meal in anticipation, but all this can easily be avoided if we focus on teaching good manners around meal times.

Having eaten, if there are any pieces of food left over that you want to give Nico, just place these in a separate bowl and keep it covered and move it somewhere so he can't get to it. Think about using a few of these treats/rewards in a very short training game ('Sit/Stay/Come/Watch,' for example) around twenty minutes after your meal and maybe use the rest in a 'Find' game in the garden. Nico will love the treats and you will both benefit far more from the exchange than if he had just scoffed the lot earlier.

What system will you practice when eating your meal? Where will your trainee be while you eat? Will you give him a kong, a treat or toy as you ask him to 'Settle' and 'Stay'? What will you do when you return to the kitchen with the leftovers? What short training game could you practice after you have eaten?

Your trainee's daily intake of food will definitely influence his state of mind each day, his physical wellbeing, his quality of life and is very likely to affect how long he will live, so please think about what you will feed him. Is there anything you want to explore about your dog's food and nutrition? What will you change about your approach to feeding and treating?

Liver Cake Recipe

Preparation:

Place 250g of lamb liver (or ox liver) in a deep(ish) dish or saucepan. Add a small splash (about 2 tablespoons) of milk. Blitz this mixture until all the liver is smooth and you're left with a semolina-like consistency. Add an egg and blend/blitz again. Then add one (heaped) cup of self-raising flour and fold in (and/or stir) until the mixture has a soup-like texture and the flour has been absorbed. Lightly grease the sides and base of an oven-proof baking dish or bread tray and/or place a baking sheet in the dish so it will be easy to tip out after cooking. Transfer the mixture to the oven-proof dish and get ready to cook!*

Cooking:

Pre-heat oven to about 170C (160C for fan oven) or gas mark 3 and then cook/bake for about 45 mins. Remove. Leave the baked cake to cool for about 20 mins before cutting it into slices and then cubes while still warm.

General:

After cooling, place some in a training dish to be used for training 'there and then'—your trainee will be waiting! Put the rest aside and place in your freezer later in small individual bags. These can be taken out and defrosted before key training times. Feel free to add some bacon bits or herbs to the recipe as well.

*Use gluten-free flour if you prefer

Cheesy Bites Recipe

Ingredients:

100g self-raising flour, 200g oats, 100g grated cheese, 1 or 2 tablespoons oil (sunflower or vegetable) and ½ cup of cold water*

Preparation:

Mix all dry ingredients together in a bowl with your hands, then add the oil and stir or mix. Add the water and you should have a very sticky cake-like mixture. Break off little bits of the mixture and roll these into small bite-sized balls and flatten slightly into tiny scone shapes. Lightly grease the base of an oven-proof baking dish and/or place a baking sheet in the dish so it will be easy to tip out after cooking. Place the tiny scones into the dish (spacing them out) and get cooking!

Cooking:

Pre-heat oven to about 180C (170C for fan oven) or gas mark 4 and cook/bake for about 20-25 mins or until the 'bites' turn a golden colour.

General:

After cooling, place some in a dish to be used for training 'there and then' and put the rest in the freezer in small individual bags, to be taken out and defrosted when needed. Consider adding some finely chopped herbs to the recipe too.

**Use gluten-free flour if you prefer*

Chapter 17

Laps and Furniture

Laps

If your dog, Pace, gets on very well with people and other dogs ... is always responsive to you and happens to regularly perch on your lap when you're watching TV—and you're happy with this arrangement—then there isn't any need to change the status quo. A happy, loving and respectful relationship is in place—give Pace lots of lap-cuddles and carry on.

If, however, you have a trainee called Miguel who often develops very selective hearing when you are out walking together and is a complete nightmare when someone comes to the front door, you might want to start asking for a little more respect at times indoors and start teaching some etiquette ... a few simple manners. One opportunity to practice 'teaching manners' might be to ask Miguel to 'Wait' for a minute or so before coming up alongside you on the chair or sofa. Once you see that his colour is favourable and he's in a waiting state, definitely invite him to come up for some cuddles at that stage. Practising some manners around 'access to the teacher' is very healthy for any trainee and quite important if yours can sometimes be a little wilful.

More than one dog

If you have more than one dog at home you may need to reconsider any pattern of 'freely jumping up on your lap.' If you are sitting on the sofa and Miguel jumps up on your lap and there are other dogs in the immediate area, you might, albeit unintentionally, be opening the door to potential conflict. Miguel can appear to others as being 'on top of' you, maybe giving off the vibe to other dogs (and people) present that he's in a strong position. Even if Miguel has no agenda at all and is just having a lovely time resting on/alongside you, his position alone can invite interest and, depending on the individual dogs, home environment and people involved, this can sometimes cause disharmony.

What to do?

If Miguel jumps up on your lap with a vibe that is positive and green and his new position doesn't affect other dogs at home, then great. Give lots of (calm) cuddles to nurture this green energy and vibe you are feeling at home. Also, tell the other trainees present that they are "Good dogs" too. Great.

If, however, this changes at any time and you feel, see or hear a change in his manner or intention, urge Miguel to move off immediately. This can be done by gently encouraging him to leave his present position by taking hold of his collar or even standing up and motivating him, gently but firmly, to move 'Off.' Once all four paws are on the floor disagree with any attempt to jump back up, remaining green, calm and in control at all times. Having waited for a couple of minutes you could invite him up on your lap again by saying, "Come on Miguel, come up here," but immediately disagree with any behaviour or vibe that appears negative. Definitely frown on any barking, posturing or growling at people or other dogs present and never just 'let it go.' You are the teacher. If a poor behaviour or colour shows itself, then remove Miguel from his lofty position once again and ensure he waits on the floor (for at least a few minutes) before restarting the invitation process. Be clear and matter-of-fact in your approach and don't change your mind, even if you get a canine look that you might interpret as 'what did I do wrong?'

If Miguel is quite 'full-on,' place a lead on him at the beginning of the exercise, as this is likely to improve your confidence levels and your ability to calmly control the situation ... have one easily at hand whenever you engage in this kind of conditioning. Praise positive colours/behaviour consistently and try not to feel guilty at all if you have to instruct your trainee. The message is clear: 'If I invite you to join me, you're very welcome to be with me; but as soon as I see behaviours or colours that are not positive, as your teacher, I'll manage the situation and calmly restore order.'

Furniture

Assuming you're quite happy with the idea of dogs resting on a sofa, chair or bed at home, then allowing them up on your furniture is absolutely fine. As mentioned already, if you have a balanced dog at home, one who's very compliant and gets on well with people and other dogs, is happy to move from your furniture whenever he's asked, then—provided other dogs at home are not affected by his new resting place—you really don't need to change your ways (or your trainee's) at all. On the other hand, you might have an adolescent dog who, for example, occasionally 'tunes you out' or a very strong-minded trainee who regularly pushes his luck and needs crystal clear boundaries at home ... or you might have a number of dogs that get into a heightened state regarding position on or near furniture, in which case you'll need to take some positive action in the home.

The strategy we've already set out for 'dogs on laps' also applies to our furniture, particularly if you have a dog with a determined mind living at home. Try to get into the habit of allowing a wilful trainee to come up onto the furniture only after you've clearly invited him. There's a very important difference—from a (strong-minded) trainee's perspective—between a case where he makes the decision to freely jump up on items and one where he has a respectful perspective and waits patiently until he's invited—the latter being the respectful approach we should nurture. Having manners should pay off for your trainee, of course, so if he starts to show a more respectful and responsive outlook in general at home and when outside, then he should get a little more freedom and easier access to you and your furniture.

If you ever want your trainee to move off an item of furniture and he's a little resistant to the idea you'll need to ask him to move using a clear and expectant teacher-like manner. Stay calm and try to remain in control of the situation. Having a lead beside the piece of furniture in question is a worthwhile idea—simply place it on your trainee whenever you want to boost your confidence and use it gently to help guide him off if necessary. It's far more effective to motivate a dog to move off the item of his own accord, so please avoid any negative lead *pulling* action here. Encourage a trainee to move 'Off' by gently guiding him using your lead to suggest the direction you want him to move in. Just use your 'Off' command while making a suitable pointing/hand gesture and remain green and determined. When he's left the item of furniture, immediately ask him to 'Wait' and then 'let him be' for a few minutes, disagreeing with any attempt to jump back up. Once your trainee is waiting patiently and respectfully, then invite him onto the chair, sofa or bed using a quiet but very positive vibe. 'Manners please!' is your key message here.

Reward good manners and green behaviour by sharing affection enthusiastically at the right time.

Chapter 18

Grooming

If you haven't groomed a dog before and want to build up your confidence levels, why not get in touch with a reputable dog groomer or your breeder? Make an appointment to visit them or invite a mobile groomer to come to your home to groom your dog with you the first few times. Hopefully, you'll be able to watch and pick up a few tips and you can get involved too at times. Some dogs, of course, have very specific needs when it comes to maintaining their long or dense coats and will need ongoing attention, so seeking some professional advice initially on a few issues will help teach you how to cater to your dog's particular coat type and you will learn how to manage it yourself in between visits to the salon. Think about buying a good breed-specific book and speak with an experienced groomer, breeder or an informed friend and get some practical advice.

The 'a little a lot' rule should be applied to basic grooming at home, building up very positive associations with the whole 'grooming event' in short bursts rather than spending ages grooming in one hit, once a month, for example. Start with a five or ten-minute session one day and practice like this every few days … gradually increasing the grooming time to about fifteen-minute sessions over time. A fifteen-minute duration doesn't sound like a lot but you really can do quite a lot of basic grooming during this time and, if you're doing this fairly regularly at home, all of these little sessions will add up to a lot.

Think ahead

Planning ahead can change the grooming experience completely for trainer and trainee. Exercising your dog beforehand, choosing a suitable place to groom, having your lead and all of your equipment ready so you won't have to stop grooming during the session, preparing a few juicy treats and playing some of your favourite music are all worth considering. Thinking ahead really does pay off and having a plan will help you feel more in control—this clarity and confidence will be passed on to your green trainee.

Positive associations

If your dog has medium or high energy levels, it's important to exercise him before you begin your grooming session so he can get rid of any pent-up energy and be able to accept this standing and waiting exercise and achieve a green frame of mind. Consider playing a short game with him before and after each grooming session too, as this will reinforce the positive association with the activity once more, so he'll be delighted the next time a brush appears.

Stay green

Each grooming session should start by putting a lead on your trainee, so you have a good level of control already in place right at the beginning. Use your commands ('Wait' and 'Settle' etc.) effectively throughout and remember to stay green should your trainee ever get distracted or exuberant during a session. Some dogs can become skilled at sabotaging stationary activities like grooming, particularly if they see them as mundane. So, remember not to give in to a trainee that's trying to call a grooming session off or deliberately trying to 'escape the event' by finding an excitable amber mindset or he'll learn quickly that he can end the session when he decides to act up in a particular way. Use distraction techniques by involving a toy or food treats very early in any grooming session and ask a family member or friend for some support too. If you do your best to make the whole activity fun and engaging, you should both start and end with green minds.

Grooming the mind

Even if you routinely take Nualla, your trainee, to your local grooming salon you should practice grooming her on your own too at times and this is also true even if your dog has a short coat that's already very manageable.

On a practical level, by completing regular short grooming sessions yourself, you will have opportunities to examine your dog's coat close-up and check for ticks or abnormalities. You will be able to ensure that Nualla has a healthy coat and you will also spot any irregularities early on. Clearly, the physical side of grooming holds great value and, just as significantly, you are also investing time 'grooming Nualla's mind.'

Use each session as an opportunity to practice various commands like 'Stand,' 'Wait' and 'Settle' and motivate Nualla to get used to being handled—having her face, paws or rear end touched, for example—while finding a relaxed state of mind. Given that each grooming activity places you in a position of 'affection giver,' 'game maker' and 'upbeat teacher,' each positive session will enhance your vibe in your trainee's mind. This increased level of respect will show itself elsewhere so 'grooming the mind' is really worthwhile, whether your trainee has a long or short coat.

Reflecting and Perfecting

Part of being a responsible teacher involves evaluating what went well and what didn't in any grooming session. Acknowledge the good parts of your existing grooming routine and definitely strive to improve too. Maybe you're having problems persistently in one area and can't figure out why. Perhaps your dog, Ash, jumps around whenever you start brushing his tail and you're very aware that he's not too keen on having his feet touched. Maybe you could try standing in a different position than you did before, focusing more on where and how you place your hands ... and be aware of how you touch—this should feel positive and 'green' to your trainee. Grooming Ash in a different place at home is worth exploring too as this shift in environment might help change his state of mind. By introducing a favourite toy or a few tasty treats into the equation here, you are likely to figure out what works best for you and Ash. Definitely ask someone experienced to observe your technique early on if you feel you need a little support. Get their opinion on what you could do differently before or during the part of your grooming routine that you're finding tricky—in this way you'll be much more confident the next time you decide to groom on your own at home.

Practising regular 'green' grooming sessions will offer much more than a nice-looking coat. Remember to 'groom the mind' regularly and try to involve other family members too. The grooming 'game' should be enjoyable for you and your trainee—it can be very therapeutic—and will give you and other family members an opportunity to teach manners and build responsiveness.

ENJOYING YOUR DOG

Chapter 19

Play and train

Game playing with your trainee offers huge benefits, aside from the obvious one of having fun with your dog. You'll be associated with these exciting times, the end result being that your trainee will be quite convinced that listening to you feels great and pays off. This positive connection will definitely improve communication skills and fuel your dog's more responsive behaviour.

When considering the kind of games to play, one factor to really focus on is your dog's level of energy. Ask yourself, does he need to burn off lots of energy or will a gentler activity be more his cup of tea? An Agility training course or a stroll in the park? Most dogs will show great interest levels in certain games and far less in others, so you'll need to study your dog's keenness or 'drive' in different activities to get a feel for what he's naturally great at and figure out what doesn't really suit him. Breed characteristics should be factored in too when you're considering suitable activities. For example, if you have a dog that's clearly designed to run like the wind, it makes sense to think of a game that will match his original purpose—one suitable game in the park might involve getting him to run after a ball or frisbee thrown at speed.

Find It

We'll explore more about game playing activities shortly, but for now, let's assume you think the 'Find' game is a good one to practice. Start in the garden or in a quiet area of a park by placing your trainee on lead and ask him to 'Sit' and 'Stay' alongside you for a minute or so. Throw a few small treats a few metres out in front of you—include some tiny pieces of finely chopped cheddar cheese, cooked chicken or cooked liver into the mix of treats as this will really motivate your trainee and keep him keen. (Use a toy or ball in place of food if you prefer.) If your dog's waiting (fairly) patiently, then un-clip or release the lead and, as you do, give an enthusiastic command to 'Find.' Most will have no problem getting to grips with this part of the routine! After he returns to you or comes in your direction with that look and body language that says, 'I've found everything,' praise him excitedly by saying, "Gooood Find."

Just enough challenge

Once you're sure he understands what 'Find' means at close quarters, you can start making the activity more interesting by throwing or placing a few treats quite a distance away and take great pleasure in watching him investigate your back garden or an area inside the home, tracking and sniffing out the goodies. Appreciate that your exhilarating vibe will make a very positive link with the activity too. If he doesn't find everything you've placed down for him initially, send him off to 'Find' again enthusiastically and take him towards any treasures he might have missed. This type of exercise will prove stimulating for most dogs and, significantly, will improve your trainee's responsiveness elsewhere; using some of his daily allocation of food to practice 'Find' is a brilliant approach.

Be inventive when thinking about where and at what level (high or low) you scatter the food. 'Just enough challenge' is a good idea at first, so your trainee is stimulated and well rewarded, gradually raising the bar once he has the idea. As mentioned, you can and should vary the lure you use in 'Find' exercises once your trainee is pretty good at 'finding' food—introduce a toy or ball as well and train him to find these items when hidden under a bush or a towel or maybe off the ground on a bench in the garden. At the end of the search—once everything's been found and picked up—say "Good Find" and finish the exercise positively by giving lots of affection. Consider clapping your hands twice (or do something similar) as well as saying "Free-time" or "Break" to signal the training activity is now complete. Then move away from the area where you've been practising. By doing this you're communicating in a very clear, fun and fair manner, making it easy for your trainee to learn quickly.

More than one dog at a time

If you have a number of dogs living together, then you could plan this activity in canine pairs, depending on 'who gets on with who' where food is concerned. Alternatively, perform the exercise initially in single file and reward each dog in turn for a successful 'Find,' eventually building up to the point where more than one dog 'hunts' at the same time. Dogs that practice this exercise together repeatedly get accustomed to searching and eating alongside each other—this will then become a familiar and positive behaviour that can help improve social skills and reduce any food aggression tendencies. Supervision is required if you have more than one dog … to help avoid any conflict arising. If you scatter mainly very small food pellets or finely diced cooked meat over quite a wide area or hide more than one toy in different places at a time, dogs are generally too busy hunting for small pickings to take too much interest in any other dog present. Also, they learn very quickly that getting assertive usually means having less hunting and eating time than others, so any older negative behaviour around food/resources can diminish quickly as a result.

Developing communication skills through play

Play, very importantly, builds up levels of confidence in dogs, young or old. If integrated into any training regime, it can prove a wonderful training aid. Regular play sessions will strengthen your bond and will really help improve mutual communication skills while having fun. You will get good at reading your trainee's vibe and his 'likes and dislikes' in play. Your trainee will learn about you too and become familiar with your vibe, colour and mannerisms when playing and get very good at listening and responding to your 'Stay,' 'Find,' 'Come' and 'Good Find' interactions over time. What kind of games do you think you might integrate into training when schooling your trainee? What would he really love to do?

Chapter 20

Fetch, Frisbee and Tug

Fetch

Breed characteristics can of course play a huge part in how naturally keen a trainee is on bringing an item back to us, but we can motivate most dogs to get interested in retrieving if we're clever in our approach. Some of you might have a gundog or retrieving breed at home, already pre-programmed to be superb at this. But other breeds and some mixed breeds can match (and surpass) retriever-level interest when fetching. The 'Fetch' game is clearly not a breed exclusive activity and might be a brilliant one for you and your trainee to practice regularly.

Bring it back

Once you've taught a reliable 'Find' or 'Seek' behaviour at home using food—as outlined earlier—start using a toy or a ball (instead of food treats) when beginning to train the 'Fetch' or 'Bring it back' behaviour.

Begin by asking your dog, Alfie, to "Sit" and "Stay" beside you—put a lead on him if you feel this will give you more control. Throw a high-value toy—you'll know what he really likes—a short distance away and then say, "Alfie, Fetch" excitedly just as you release him. As your trainee approaches the toy, reissue the verbal cue in a very excited tone of voice. When he picks it up, immediately ask him to "Come" using a heightened tone and, when he does, ask Alfie to "Sit" and "Leave" (or "Drop") the toy (see *VALUABLE COMMANDS*). Accept the toy, ball or dumb-bell and then immediately praise him. If you get a successful 'Fetch' behaviour, it's a good idea to be quite exuberant early in the training process by saying something like, "Whoop, whoop! Goooood Fetch" excitedly to signal that you're ecstatic with his behaviour. Consolidate any learning by practising a few more successful retrieves and then shift your focus to something else.

Not bringing it back

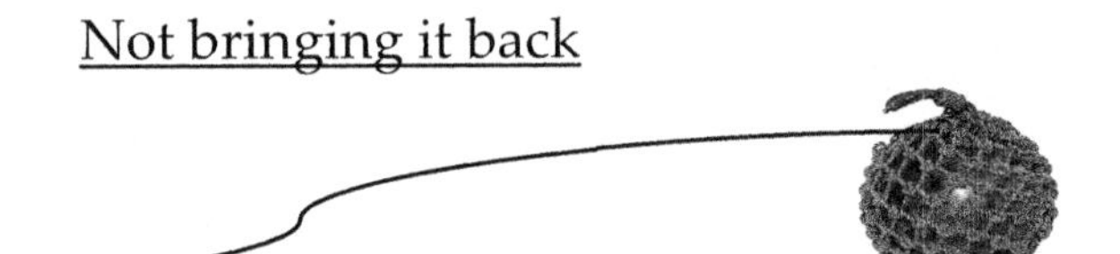

Your trainee might get into the habit of chasing after a ball or toy, picking it up enthusiastically, but then might not always bring the item all the way back to you. A simple strategy that often helps is to get some netting—the net bag that onions are sold in is a good example—and wrap this around the ball or toy. Wrap it really tightly and gather the excess netting up by twisting it at the top of the toy. Cut off much of the excess netting above the ball. Then get a long piece of string, say about four meters or so, and tie one end to the netting at the top of the toy, making it secure. Once the piece of string is firmly attached, play the 'Fetch' game again. This time, hold onto one end of the string as you throw the toy/ball a short distance away. Just as your trainee goes to investigate the 'new' item, if he looks less than keen, jerk or pull the string sharply so the ball darts as he approaches it—this is likely to motivate him to chase and pick it up. Once he picks it up relax any tension in the string and get him really excited by saying "Come" in an upbeat manner as he returns. If he drops the item on his way back to you, simply jerk the line again or reel it back in, encouraging him to 'Fetch' it again if you need to. Condition your trainee to understand the 'Fetch' game as: A) Move quickly towards the item, B) Pick it up, C) Bring the item back and D) Drop it, before being praised and restarting the game. If your trainee is uneasy about the idea of the netting covering the ball and seems less interested in playing 'Fetch' like this, simply buy a 'ball on a rope' toy and attach your long piece of string to the rope section—then try the above strategy again and your trainee should quickly get the idea.

More than one lure

One common issue that crops up when training the retrieve behaviour is that, after a while, your dog might decide he'll not surrender the article or toy that he fetches, or sometimes he won't come back to you straight away. One solution here is to have another item—a frisbee, ball or treat—waiting for your trainee as he returns. When he's picked up an item and turns and moves towards you, show him that you have something waiting for him by pushing it out in front of you. He'll immediately see you have something else on offer and (hopefully) bound towards you to exchange the one he's carrying. Don't just offer the next toy straight away but ask for some positive behaviour first like 'Leave' (or 'Drop') ... and 'Wait,' before playing 'Fetch' again. Repeat the pattern of getting another toy ready to engage him on his return.

Dogs can learn quickly from others

If your dog is consistently 'not getting it' or is a little less responsive than you want, try practising with a friend and their dog (provided their dog's already good at 'Fetch'), as one trainee will often learn more quickly from watching and imitating another in action. With your trainee on-lead, ask the other person to practice 'Fetch' with their dog a few times. Then give it a go with your trainee. If this still isn't working very well, try letting your dog go just after the other dog moves to retrieve, so that he'll follow his movement to the toy and back to you, getting the idea through copying and repetition. You may want to try throwing two toys at the same time too as this can help motivate the trainees while avoiding too much competition creeping into the game.

Integrate 'Fetch' into daily walks

As outlined earlier, one tip to promoting good 'Fetch' technique is to go to a spacious area of a park and, as you walk around with your *on-lead* trainee, casually drop a ball or a toy—one he really likes—on the ground just behind you; you'll know what lure will work best to stimulate your dog. Then start to move away from the spot and continue on the walk. Your dog is very likely to want to stop and go back for the item as you walk on using your enthusiastic "Close" or "Heel" command. Once you're about twenty metres away from it, ask your trainee to "Wait" and "Sit." Position him facing the 'lost item' and release him, saying "Fetch" excitedly. If you play this game regularly, your trainee will know exactly what to expect and you can gradually increase the distance of the retrieve—most dogs love it. Using a clear visual and verbal 'Come' command alongside excited praise on his return means great associations are being nurtured. It would be a great idea to integrate your whistle sound into this game too, so get ready to blow it just as he picks up the item and starts to move in your direction.

Professional advice

If you want to perfect your 'Fetch' technique even further, consider asking a local reputable dog trainer—maybe a gundog trainer—to meet with you and your trainee, so you can get some sound practical advice.

'Fetch' is a very valuable and enjoyable exercise to practice with most dogs, helping to lower a trainee's energy levels quite quickly while you have fun, build responsiveness and gain lots of respect through play. Try to practice the 'Fetch' game fairly often—most dogs can't get enough.

Frisbee

When you produce a frisbee for the first time, try to act in a very excited way, saying "Lola, what's this?"—clearly giving off the vibe that this new toy definitely represents playtime. Allow Lola to mouth and play with it for a short time. Once she's investigated the frisbee, find an enclosed garden or a quiet area of your local park and ask Lola to "Sit" and "Stay" in the usual manner. Then, without too much delay, say "Lola, Fetch" excitedly as you throw the frisbee in the air and let her go. Try to throw it initially so she has a fair chance of catching it mid-air, a behaviour she'll probably find very exhilarating. Once Lola's got the frisbee, call her back to you and reward in the usual way while asking her to "Wait" and "Leave/Drop" ... and then start the game again.

Use an experienced dog to motivate

If you know someone with a dog already trained to 'Fetch' a frisbee—sometimes called 'disc dogs'—then so much the better. This dog can be an excellent example for Lola—she will be motivated by the energy given off by the more experienced frisbee fanatic, so you should value this. Practice with the other handler and dog, asking them to go first and then you try it ... and keep going until you've achieved your goal. Sometimes, provided you're confident that jealousy isn't going to disrupt proceedings, it's useful to let your dog go just after the more experienced dog flies off to get the frisbee. You could also throw two frisbees, one after the other, and vary your approach according to your knowledge of your trainees and the colours you see in front of you.

Use a different disc

If you have a dog who isn't very keen on the more common 'hard plastic' frisbee then try using a rubber one instead. Many dogs really love the texture of one and not the other so you might need to experiment a little to find one that suits your trainee. For any smaller dog—who might find a standard sized frisbee a bit on the unwieldy side—choose a similar disc-toy that's more in keeping with his size, inventing your own miniature frisbee game.

Before long, you'll be able to play this game before setting off for work, when exercising your dog in the park, or when draining energy before guests arrive at home or simply whenever you want to have fun with your trainee.

Tug

'Tug-of-War' or 'Tug' is a natural game played by puppies and (some) older dogs among themselves by grappling with or 'tugging' on an item like an old towel, rope, rag or toy at home. This type of activity presents great advantages—young trainees get accustomed to engaging with other dogs at close quarters while getting a thorough workout and toning up different muscle groups. They also discover how to manipulate an article and how much force they need to use to hang onto it while figuring out how to play appropriately with others. If you have more than one dog at home, enjoy seeing them have 'Tug' fun together but apply good common sense and always supervise their interactions, so you can establish boundaries in playtime should canine minds ever start to travel into a negative colour.

In addition to being a very useful game for many dogs to engage in with fellow doggy playmates, many people play 'Tug' with their trainee too to promote good behaviour when training. Your dog, Bailey, might be offered a 'Tug' game after a few 'Sit, Stay, Come' practice sessions or Bailey might get a short 'Tug' game to help reward his responsive behaviour after completing an Agility course to keep that feel-good factor going. Many people might also play 'Tug' with Bailey at home just to have some (mutual) fun ... this is often a trainee's—and trainer's—favourite game. So, it's clear that 'Tug' can be a very useful 'go to' place for many owners when game playing and teaching ... one your trainee is likely to love ... but you might need to keep a watchful eye on a few things.

Keeping an eye

Playing 'Tug' can occasionally trigger an excited (mid/high amber) mind in some trainees, where elements of intense growling, mouthing and biting can easily creep in.

Let's say that your dog, Charlie, really loves 'Tug,' but really 'loses his marbles' when playing it, travelling from green to high amber in only a few seconds. As his teacher, it probably would be best if you didn't play 'Tug' with Charlie, or limit your play-time at least. Instead, maybe offer an alternative game you can play together that won't bring him into this negative colour. Your other dog, Lucy, is a very different kettle of fish and, while she also loves the 'Tug' game, it's clear from what you see in her eyes and her general vibe that she remains green or low amber throughout the game, even though she does play-grumble, gets excited and really goes for it! In Lucy's case, there's no need to change anything, given that no negative colour is being presented—keep playing 'Tug' with her … provided Charlie isn't nearby!

Is winning important?

An old phrase relating to playing 'Tug' with your dog was to 'always win the game,' which meant whoever was playing tug with a dog should always end up with the toy at the end. If an owner claimed or 'won' the toy at the end of playtime, it was thought they were sending the clear message to their trainee that *they* were in charge of proceedings … not the other way around.

Some research now suggests that a person 'winning the game' at the end might not be terribly relevant. Dogs tend to view 'playing Tug with people' differently to 'playing Tug with other dogs' ... most are not at all bothered about 'winning the toy' when playing with people and have no underpinning agenda at all, other than keeping the (fabulous) game going. With some dogs, however, winning at Tug and 'owning' seems to be much more important!

A good general approach is to observe the vibe and colour you are getting/seeing during playtime and adjust your interactions accordingly. If your dog, Lucy, plays 'Tug' with you using a very positive colour and vibe then it isn't important for you to finish by 'winning' and taking the toy at the end ... Lucy is having a lovely time, even though she might sound like she's in attack mode! If, however, you have a trainee like Charlie at home—one who gets very heightened during your 'Tug' games—it might be a good idea to limit the amount of time you invest in playing 'Tug' so he doesn't practice regularly going into a negative colour during playtime and regard this as a welcome state of mind.

Experiment a little and consider whether 'Tug' is the right game to play with *your* trainee or if you should limit the amount of time you play it ... or maybe stop playing it altogether. If you think this *is* a suitable game for your dog, really enjoy the game and remember to offer 'Tug' when teaching and rewarding very good behaviour as well—presenting that extra special treat for a job well done!

Chapter 21

Roller Blading, Cycling, Running and Swimming

High-energy activities will almost certainly be great fun for all taking part, particularly if your trainee has lots of energy to burn off.

Roller Blading, Cycling and Running

Confidence first

If you intend going roller-blading, cycling or running with your dog, try to bring a calm and confident attitude to the table. The common-sense approach is to only practice those activities with your dog that you're already good at. For example, if you're not an accomplished cyclist, then it's sensible to get some practice in yourself before you try to condition your trainee to walk and run alongside you in a relaxed manner. If you're learning to roller-blade and are also trying to teach your dog to run alongside you, you're obviously setting yourself and your dog up for a frustrating and super-stressful experience.

If, however, you're already very confident and comfortable with the idea of having your dog travel alongside you as you roller-blade, cycle or run, then go for it. Introduce each activity in short sessions initially so that confidence levels grow steadily as you learn together rather than setting off on a long trip straight away.

Keep that lead smiling

Try to pay attention to your trainee's position relative to you when you're cycling, roller-blading or running. Disagree with any major 'pulling forward' movement on your trainee's part. Use your 'Ah-Ah' sound if the lead does go taut, asking him to quickly come into a safe 'Close' position alongside. Nurture good behaviour by praising verbally at times and really focus on relaxing your lead when you can, so your trainee feels a comfortable and confident vibe from you when he's behaving well alongside.

Exception to the rule

Canicross (or CaniX) is a sport involving running with your dog—usually cross (X) country or off-road. The human part of the partnership wears a waist-belt with a two-metre bungee line attached to a padded dog harness. The activity provides a physical workout for both human and canine trainee, encouraging the dog to run and pull out in front of his owner while you both run at speed. Given that your trainee is often pulling out ahead of you during this activity, this is an exception to the usual 'smiling lead' guideline. The use of directional commands in Canicross teaches a dog to use his brain while working/running with his human at speed, often over rough terrain. If Canicross sounds like your cup of tea, why not do an internet search for a training group near you?

Common sense applies

As these activities can be quite vigorous, please be sensible and practice safely. If you're thinking about roller-blading with your dog, make sure you have the right protective equipment. If you intend to run or cycle with your dog, always carry some water for both and don't practice if it's hot. Rather than making a long list of *Dos and Don'ts* here, please apply good common sense ... 1) think ahead, 2) exercise with other people and their dogs and 3) have a great time with your trainee.

Swimming

Some breeds are likely to take to water more quickly than others but most can be encouraged to at least get their feet wet. Investing time motivating your trainee to go doggy-paddling and swimming can be very worthwhile, particularly if you live by the sea or near a lake, as this is a fun-filled form of exercise that you might like to practice fairly regularly.

Do your research and choose a place where the water is fairly still and the environment safe, with easy entry and exit points for your trainee. Also, ask a friend with a dog that loves water to join you—he's likely to influence your trainee positively and quickly. Play the 'Fetch' game using a ball, frisbee or floating toy within the swimming exercise too, to really make any water activity a 'wow!' experience.

Join him

Some owners say that swimming with their dog gives them an earthy or primal connection and presents great relationship benefits when out of the water. Some people prefer to paddle on the water's edge while their trainee is having the time of his life in and around water but, whatever suits you, he will almost certainly love that you're joining in the 'water game' … this presents great value. If you have a safe place to swim or paddle with your trainee, why not give it a go? Using his favourite ball, (floating) toy, frisbee or dummy as part of a game will definitely present value too.

Persuasion not pressure

Allow any young, fearful or reticent trainee time—lots of this—to get accustomed to any new game near or in the water. If your trainee is slow to 'take to water,' maybe invite friends with their dogs into the picture too—only include friendly and balanced trainees—to help build up your trainee's confidence levels steadily. Very soon, he should grow to love the experiences in and around water.

Safety matters

As mentioned already, please screw on your common-sense head here:

- Choose a safe place to have fun
- Always swim with someone else
- Don't let your dog swim in dirty, green, blue-green or very cold water
- Have towels ready—for you and your trainee—so neither of you are dripping wet for long periods. If it's really cold then 'dab' towel-dry rather than 'scrub-dry' your trainee
- Remember to bring drinking water, particularly if exercising your dog at the seaside
- Think ahead and have a great time

Chapter 22

Obedience Training

Attending an obedience training course offers great rewards —you should do your homework first by searching for a local school and trainers you will have confidence in. Speak with fellow doggy people and ask them who they recommend. Take into account factors such as the trainer's experience, cost, location, lesson times, activities used and size of class before you decide. What's right for one person might not suit you or your trainee, so make contact with and visit a couple of training groups before making an informed choice. So, why is joining a good training group so useful?

Learning from others

Some owners can be unaware of how their own vibe, handling skills, body language and tone of voice might be influencing their trainee's behaviour. Often, with only a small amount of guidance, owners can quickly see how to modify their approach by holding the lead in a particular way, changing how they stand or altering their pace while walking their dog, etc. In this way, we can all benefit from someone else observing our behaviour and giving us tips to help modify and improve our training and handling techniques. Also, you will see and hear other people getting advice and learn from what they're doing or not doing—just being around others and observing what's happening around you will add so much value.

Information sharing

Training classes are also useful in that they offer a great opportunity to find out about pretty much anything dog-related. You might have questions about head collars or various leads and can often check these items out in classes and try them on your trainee. Lessons will also provide information on activities taking place locally such as dog shows, obedience competitions, local charitable events and group walks, so you are likely to feel much more informed and supported if you attend a reputable training group.

Social benefits

As well as learning and practising some parts of the training syllabus like 'Sit' and 'Stay', we (humans) really benefit from meeting others too. Exchanging stories alongside 'problems and solutions' can be really useful. You'll also learn to appreciate that other people are experiencing similar issues to you (which can be very comforting!) and be able to see first-hand how they're teaching their dogs and modifying behaviour. These human interactions can provide great sources of information and support and you'll have lots of fun along the way. You're almost certainly going to meet like-minded people and some can make long-lasting friendships in training classes, so consider joining a good group.

Confidence

A good training class is likely to encourage you to handle other people's dogs and in return, other people might handle yours, only for a few minutes at a time. This will boost your own confidence and skillset when handling dogs in general and your resulting positive attitude will motivate your trainee to be much more responsive. His confidence will also grow as he'll understand quickly that he should behave in the same way, no matter who's handling him ... and he'll get lots of praise and the odd treat thrown in for good behaviour. You'll pick up tips from people who might handle your trainee effortlessly and recognise areas where other owners could improve with their dogs too. Some people also adopt a buddy system, where two or more owners agree to meet up and walk their dogs together during the week, thereby promoting strong canine—and human—socialisation skills on an ongoing basis.

A responsive trainee

Your trainee will obviously learn new commands by attending training classes and, significantly, will learn to practice these behaviours—like 'Sit/Stay/Come'—when dogs and people are nearby and other distractions such as smells and noises are present. Building up and practising responsiveness in an environment like a training group is a very important part of your dog's education and shouldn't be underestimated.

Role-play

If make-believe or role-play activities are introduced in training sessions in a light-hearted and fun way, they really can be brilliant teaching and learning tools. Helping your trainee become familiar with items like buggies or wheelchairs, doing 'pretend visits to the vet' where your dog experiences light-hearted mock examinations are examples of role-play exercises that can present great value. All the time your trainee is being educated to know what's expected of him in varied situations, enjoying lots of affection and getting a few tasty treats as he learns. These confidence-building experiences can prove invaluable, particularly when similar events happen for real.

Pride

Most people take great pride in their trainee and are very keen to see him learn, enjoy himself and progress quickly. Owners attending training lessons—usually for an hour each week—are sure to strive to achieve weekly goals set by trainers and demonstrate their progression in forthcoming lessons. This is a great outlook, one that will help motivate and encourage any owner to practice training techniques consistently in between training lessons, resulting in a very well-schooled trainee.

Progression route

You'll also be able to progress through different training milestones as most good training groups offer Beginner,

Intermediate and Advanced training levels. Later on, you might even consider taking part in competitions, if this interests you. After a time, once you have a good training foundation in place, you'll be in a better position to assess what your dog really enjoys and can start thinking about what you'd like to do in the future. Given that your trainee (having attended training classes) will have a solid grounding in obedience and socialisation you'll be able to use this as a springboard to join higher level obedience training classes or you might prefer to join an Agility, Flyball, Gundog or a Scent-work training group, for example.

The key message—even if your dog is already a great listener and an absolute angel at home—is to consider joining a reputable training course.

Chapter 23

Agility, Flyball and Ringcraft

Agility

An Agility course is made up of many obstacles that must be navigated by a dog in sequence (obstacle #1 is followed by #2, then #3 etc.) by listening to direction from his owner/handler. Courses can be designed to be simple, challenging or *very* challenging according to the level of the participants. Many people enrol in fun Agility classes to have a great time with their dog at their own pace, while others look for a competitive club as they want to try their hand at completing more complex courses against the clock. You must choose what will really suit you and your trainee.

Many groups have a foundation level or some pre-Agility lessons on offer so you can 'test the water' and progress gradually. Courses are altered for smaller breeds too to suit their size, so don't be put off if you have a small dog that might love and excel at Agility.

Common challenges

You will be challenged (mentally and physically) on an Agility course, as it will be up to you to move/run alongside your dog—guiding him to the next obstacle at just the right moment while trying to remember the course! Getting your dog to 'Weave' in and out between short vertical poles, go 'Through' tunnels and tyres and leap 'Over' jumps set up in different places on a course are all common Agility commands and activities, and there are many other skills you and your trainee will learn too.

Gauging levels of interest

Some people buy or make up a small selection of Agility obstacles for the garden so they can practice at home. Some use a child's hula-hoop—along with a ball or toy—to practice going 'Through.' Others buy or make a few jumps as well to give their trainee the idea of what's expected when practising the 'Over' command. These obstacles can prove a great way of helping you gauge how interested you and your trainee are likely to be in Agility before you consider joining a training group.

Age matters

Dogs need to be at least a year old before they'll be considered by most Agility training groups. Some clubs do invite slightly younger dogs to attend foundation lessons where good technique is taught rather than practising any exuberant running/jumping/turning. This ensures the level of activity your trainee will be involved in won't adversely affect his physical health. Many Agility clubs recommend a young dog attends obedience classes while he is developing, so he gets good at practising useful commands like 'Wait,' 'This way,' 'Come,' etc. and, significantly, learns to be responsive to his handler when around other dogs. This solid grounding will prove invaluable when your trainee begins Agility training.

Benefits

Agility training classes will suit some owners and dogs more than others but these are likely to be great fun for you and your trainee, are a great way to improve fitness levels (for human and canine) and will help build responsivity and your mutual bond. Most dogs really love it, as it gives them an opportunity to move at pace while listening to and following direction—exciting! So, if Agility training appeals to you and you think your dog would love it, why not visit a couple of local groups and think about joining one that suits you.

Flyball

This sport can be a great one to consider if you have a dog with speed on his side. As with Agility, there are usually introductory or foundation courses available to help you develop some basic skills and assess if this is the right activity for you and your dog.

How it works

In a competition setting, each Flyball team consists of four handlers—each person with one dog—and two teams compete against each other at any one time. Two identical courses are prepared and each team begins by assembling behind their starting point. Each competitor gets organised according to their running order—first, second, third or fourth. Once the 'green light' has been given, the first handler on both teams sends out 'dog number one.' Each dog runs in a straight line over a series of low hurdles towards a Flyball box which 'magically' ejects a tennis ball when a dog touches a sensitive spring-loaded pad with his front paws. Each dog hopes to eject and grab the ball and return at speed over the hurdles in the direction of his handler. Once over the finish line, the second dog is released and the relay continues until the first 'dog number four' returns. The winning team is announced once finishing times and any penalties have been calculated.

Age

Dogs need to be around a year old before they're considered by any reputable Flyball training group. Just as with Agility or any other exhilarating sport, this age guideline exists to protect a juvenile's physical health from being adversely affected.

Skills to perfect

As you'll appreciate, Flyball is really suited to dogs who like to run and jump. This sport challenges a dog's concentration levels when there's quite a lot going on around them and, while it is less physically demanding for people than Agility, you will need to work hard to develop sound handling skills. These include knowing exactly when to release your dog; teaching your trainee to pass by other dogs at speed; training him how to eject/catch the ball from the box and how to turn most effectively once he has it; and you will need to work as an effective team member.

If you think Flyball might suit you and your trainee, consider looking online to get some additional information and then think about viewing a local training session—without your dog initially—so you can speak with someone who will be able to advise on how you can get involved.

Ringcraft

If you're thinking about showing your dog or want more information then attending a good Ringcraft class is a sound idea. Experienced show-goers and breeders will be present and happy to advise on 'how things work,' explaining Kennel Club regulations and show terminology. Classes will teach you how to improve your handling skills and your trainee will learn what's involved and what he needs to do too.

How things work

Group training sessions will encourage you to rehearse the finer points of Ringcraft as though you were taking part in a mock-show. Trainers will teach you how to motivate and lure your trainee to move alongside you at the correct pace and condition him to stand in one position while someone 'goes over' or examines him. Significantly, your dog will learn to listen to you while other people and unfamiliar dogs are in the immediate area. Your goal will be to show him off in the very best light so you'll really benefit from some expert guidance on how to get the best out of your trainee in the ring. You'll practice showing your dog while moving in a straight line and then travel in a circular and a triangular formation and experience what it's like to be observed and judged in a show ring … and hopefully become more confident and skilful, knowing exactly what to expect when you compete in a real show.

Young and old

Puppies and older dogs alike can join Ringcraft classes. Puppies will need to be around six months of age to start training but some enthusiasts prefer to get started even sooner than this and put a lot of work in at home while their puppy is very young, so any handling and standing exercises become familiar and automatic for their trainee. Think about talking with your breeder to get some advice and make contact with a local Ringcraft training group—they will explain how you can get started with your particular trainee.

Added benefits

Lessons usually run once a week for an hour or so and these can offer a great social outlet too as you'll meet up with people with similar interests. Some might have the same breed of dog as yours so you probably will have a lot to chat about! You will also be able to watch others run/show their dogs and are likely to learn a lot from this experience. If you have a show quality dog, consider learning the ropes and have fun with him by joining a good Ringcraft group.

Chapter 24

Gundog Training

Dogs that traditionally work 'in the field' tend to fall into three categories: pointers, springers and retrievers. In simple terms, pointers are trained to search for and 'point' at particular game, springers 'spring' game up from dense cover and retrievers 'retrieve' game found on the ground or in water.

Solid foundations

Some dogs are natural 'multipurpose dogs,' able and keen to do every task—hunt, point and retrieve—very well, while many others are better at sticking to one discipline they always do to a very high standard. The type of work you intend to do with your trainee will depend, of course, on his breeding and natural 'drive' or keenness in particular activities. If you have a dog that loves retrieving and performs brilliantly on open ground, an instructor is likely to start you and your trainee off by perfecting skills in this environment before moving on to other more complex tasks and settings.

Responsiveness

Field activities really stimulate a dog, but he must be seen to be under your control when he hears or sees game moving or when he hears a shot. A common instruction to give a dog is to 'mark' prey as they fall or scatter, so he knows where to look for them after shots have been fired. Many handlers will practice their 'quartering' skills too, where a dog is used as a tracker and springer of game, all the time moving left and right in front of his handler but not veering off too far in any one direction, with the intention of pushing up any game as he travels. Other dogs are asked to practice a number of retrieves over very different terrain while listening to directional commands from the handler.

As you can see, these exercises capitalise on and use a gundog's intelligence, his agility on land and in water, his scenting and listening skills and, significantly, he's practising being responsive to his handler while having the time of his life, so he's very likely to listen to you elsewhere as well.

Dummies

Even if you have little or no interest in taking up hunting or shooting yourself, if you have a gundog breed, you can still practice at home and in training sessions using dummies or on real game shot by someone else. Group training classes will give you the opportunity to practice your verbal, visual and whistle commands while other people and their trainees are nearby, so you and your dog are likely to get a lot from these sessions. He'll almost certainly love going to outdoor training classes and it will be great for you to see him happy in his work too.

Most training groups offer a means of progression through various training levels over time, where you and your trainee gradually become more accomplished in different activities. Once you've been practising for a while and you've built up your skills, you might realise (as many do) that you have 'the gundog bug!' You could consider training for and entering some working tests and then field trial competitions where you and your trainee can have fun meeting with and competing against others. If you have a gundog breed at home and would like to get involved, think about making contact with a reputable training group near you.

Chapter 25

Tracking and SAR

Practising a little at home

A basic strategy to kick-start basic tracking training might be to start a young trainee off by asking him to 'Find' food treats or articles hidden in the garden and then gradually expand this mind-set so he learns to apply this behaviour to 'finding his human' outdoors too. Try keeping your trainee, Mimi, on-lead and ask a family member to give Mimi a little cooked chicken or liver cake just before leaving and running away from her excitedly. Ask them to take themselves into the garden or another room and quickly use your "Mimi, Find" instruction as you lead her to them i.e. she tracks them down. One she 'finds' the person, Mimi should be given a reward immediately and she will inevitably love this search game. Start off slowly to make sure Mimi finds the 'missing person' fairly easily and gradually increase the level of challenge.

Making contact with a tracking group

Assuming Mimi is loving each and every search 'game' at home and in the park, then it might be a good idea to make contact with a local working or tracking group. These groups will run regular tracking training sessions and you will get some clear guidance on how to train Mimi to find varied objects or follow scents laid down in different environments. Tracking exercises are usually completed outdoors on foot, so training is great fun for trainer and trainee alike. It takes a lot of time, effort and commitment to get really good at tracking, but it's a fascinating and rewarding activity to get involved in. While Mimi is likely to love every single tracking outing, she will also find it quite draining mentally, so you will have a much more contented dog living at home as a result of working her like this. You will be associated with these fabulous times and Mimi should be more responsive to you. If tracking sounds like an ideal activity for you and your trainee, why not complete an online search for 'dog tracking training' in your area? This should return results that will get you started. (You might also like to research 'Scentwork for dogs.')

Taking tracking very seriously

Your local area will almost certainly have a well-established Search and Rescue (SAR) group with the serious job of finding missing people or items dropped by people on the move, often helping police forces when weather conditions are poor, when terrain is difficult or if an official search spans a large area. A SAR team survives primarily on the excellent commitment of their volunteers and their very well-trained Search and Rescue dogs. If your dog has a brilliant nose and you both really love 'Find' games outdoors and you are very keen to get involved, why not contact your local SAR organisation? They will be able to tell you how your dog can be assessed and explain the process.

Chapter 26

Lure Coursing

Lure coursing is where dogs run after or 'hunt' a dummy prey item rather than any live animal. The artificial lure—often a white rag, a fake squirrel tail or something else that looks inviting—is pulled along the ground on a wire at speed, operated by someone controlling a motorised system. Courses are designed to mirror older live coursing events, pegged out to challenge those taking part. A course might be laid out in a straight-line format for young dogs who'll run after a lure without too many sharp turns or bends—allowing them time to learn their craft safely. Once the trainees have got the idea, a sharp bend can be introduced and then a triangular course will need a lot of practice. Over time you'll learn what distance your trainee is best at and can get some advice and support from experienced trainers on how to really bring him up to speed! If you have a dog who loves to run and chase, finding a lure coursing club near you might be worth investigating.

Breed specific?

Each training session will challenge each dog's speed, fitness, endurance and agility in turns while fulfilling an inner need to run and 'hunt' at pace alongside other dogs. Greyhounds, Italian Greyhounds, Whippets, Wolfhounds,

Deerhounds, Salukis and many other 'running breeds' are usually extremely keen to join in this chasing game, but lure coursing is not exclusive to sighthounds or pure breeds alone. If you have 'Mr or Mrs Speedy' at home and think you would like to find out more, most clubs will be very happy to help and advise you. Maybe you can chat with someone who is already taking part and arrange to go along with them to take a look at a training session?

<u>Local club guidelines apply</u>

Due to the physical demands of the sport, dogs usually need to be over a year old before any serious lure coursing training begins. This age guideline will depend on your local club's rules and training regime. The number of dogs each one runs against, the number of turns involved, how turns are arranged and the distances covered will all depend on your dog's age, size, breed and experience, as well as the training methods and preferences of those running your local club. Dogs are generally raced in 'braces' (twos) or 'trios' (threes) where similar breeds usually race against each other. Once your dog has become pretty good at chasing lures in practice, you can start focusing on one particular discipline … so he gets used to one format and becomes really accomplished at running/chasing over a set course and distance.

If you have a trainee that you think is really made for this, consider searching online for a 'lure coursing club' or 'sighthound lure coursing' or 'longdog club' near you to find out how you can get involved. Your trainee is likely to love this type of hunting simulation and stimulation and you, of course, will be closely associated with it. As a result, you will have a more contented and responsive dog living at home.

Chapter 27

Therapy Dogs

You may already have seen a Therapy dog visiting people in a hospital or a retirement/nursing home—these volunteers (human and canine) offer great comfort and support to people and are increasingly being recruited to motivate and stimulate those with varied learning difficulties in schools/education, proving to be of significant benefit for most who interact with them. Many recipients of a therapy dog's attention and affection become more relaxed, engage more easily and their mental wellbeing improves as a result of the loving interaction and contact he brings. So, it really is a privilege to work with your trainee and give so much happiness to others at the same time. I think you'll agree, if we ever have to spend a little time in hospital or know of someone dear to us in a nursing or retirement home, a visiting volunteer with their canine—wagging tail in tow—would surely bring a smile to all of our faces.

Temperament

A sound temperament is obviously a paramount requirement when working out if this kind of activity is one that would suit your dog. A therapy dog needs to really enjoy meeting and being stroked affectionately by people of different ages and like the idea of sitting quietly beside someone in bed or being fussed by someone in a chair. Your trainee will need to be comfortable when approached by people using walking frames and wheelchairs and be unphased by uniformed personnel or other unusual smells or noises he is likely to encounter when visiting and 'doing his rounds'.

If you have a dog that's very confident and pretty relaxed in whatever situation he finds himself in, always keen for human affection and quite responsive to direction from you, and you want to help others by working with him—showing off his wonderful nature at the same time—then this is something you could explore.

Age

In general, therapy dog organisations won't consider a dog for assessment until they are at least a year old. This is to ensure that your trainee has a certain level of maturity—mentally and physically—before placing him in a fairly challenging and responsible role like this.

Getting involved

The general procedure is to find a leading 'therapy dog' organisation by doing some research online—check out a few and, if you are quite keen on one, make contact to find out more. You will be asked to complete and submit some online forms and, once these have been processed, a meeting with your local therapy dog assessor can be arranged. The assessor's role is to see if you and your dog are a team that's really suited to this kind of voluntary work and check how steady your dog is in different situations.

If you and your dog are successful in your assessment, you will both be approved as a volunteer therapy dog team and you can start thinking about who you would like to visit and support—maybe patients in a local hospital or nursing home or students in a nearby school?

VALUABLE COMMANDS

As mentioned earlier when talking about the 'Essential Commands,' it's really important to teach some key behaviours very early in life so our trainees clearly understand what we want them to do and know how to behave at different times. The following section outlines how you can build up your command set even further and teach a few more valuable behaviours like:

- Watch
- Down
- Leave
- This Way
- Stand

*Search for **LoveK9 TV** on YouTube to view our **Watch** video*

Chapter 28

Watch

Look at me and focus on me

Being able to ask your dog to make eye contact with you and focus on you can be really useful, especially when there are distractions nearby.

Look into my eyes

The easiest way to train this behaviour is to ask your dog to sit in front of you, facing you. Place a lure—a juicy treat, a favourite toy or ball—in your hand and make a fist. Then extend your index finger and place your fist (with the lure) near your trainee's nose. He'll start investigating your hand straight away, at which point you should give your verbal "Watch" before bringing your index finger from your dog's nose back towards your face and eyes. His eyes will follow the direction of your index finger—staying keen on the lure, of course—and he should end up looking into your eyes intently as a result.

Give your "Watch" command again and, provided your trainee is now staring at you intently, reward this positive behaviour quickly by giving the treat or toy and a verbal "Goooood Watch" very enthusiastically. Remember, your goal is for him to *hold his gaze on you* when you give the command, rather than looking at you and then glancing away again.

Progress steadily

Use high value treats initially to really help condition the new behaviour—small pieces of cooked liver, chicken or cheese are all good choices. Gradually extend the amount of 'watching' time you ask for, starting off with a few seconds and then working up to ten seconds of 'watching you' before you reward.

Raising the bar

You'll need to repeat short practice 'Watch' sessions a number of times before he starts to get the idea that he should look into your eyes and hold his gaze on you when he hears the verbal 'Watch' cue and sees your clear visual cue—your index finger moving back towards your face. Once your trainee consistently reacts successfully to your 'Watch' instruction, start *gradually* increasing the amount of 'Watch' time from ten seconds of 'watching' to fifteen and even twenty before rewarding.

Use the 'Watch' alongside other commands

Once he's pretty good at the exercise you can build the 'Watch' into a sequence of behaviours. You could, for example, use short combinations like, 'Wait, Sit, Stay and Watch' and then reward after a short time. Creating routines in this way will help condition *you* to use your new instructions automatically too. Practice regularly by applying the 'a little a lot' rule, as you don't want to say the word so much that your dog gets tired of the activity and begins to look elsewhere.

When or where can it be used?

The 'Watch' command can be used effectively when your trainee becomes very focused on other dogs, on something else across the street or in the park, or in any situation where he's generally not paying much attention to you. If he tends to stalk other dogs when he's out walking on lead, as soon as you spot any negative colour creeping in, use your 'Wait, Sit, Watch' combination until the distraction has passed by. Once the distraction has moved on say something like 'Free-time' or 'Break' to indicate the end of the 'Watch' exercise. Motivate with treats or another lure to cultivate good behaviour.

A further benefit of this training combination will become clear when you and your dog are in a confined space—like sitting in a café or in your vet's waiting room. Your trainee will neither trigger responses in any other dog nearby nor receive any that might cause misbehaviours, given that his focus will be on you when 'Watching'. You can reinforce this behaviour by giving positive verbal feedback and quietly stroke your trainee on the head, under the chin or behind the ears ... with the occasional food treat, keeping him motivated to maintain the 'Watch' position. It's an easy command to train at home and has great value, so it's well worth teaching early on.

Chapter 29

Down

Put your tummy on the floor

Some people use the word 'down' automatically in the context of 'Get down from the sofa!' or 'Get down—stop jumping up at me!' If this sounds like familiar behaviour to you—in order to avoid any confusion for your trainee—you might prefer to use another word like saying "Flat" when training this 'tummy on floor' behaviour.

<u>Between the paws</u>

Most dogs find going from a standing position to a 'Down' in one movement fairly unnatural, so begin training the 'Down' behaviour by asking your trainee, Sally, to 'Sit' initially. Once in a steady 'Sit' right in front of you, place a few treats in your hand—Sally will probably be very keen to investigate! Keep the treats near her nose for a few seconds while keeping your palm facing the ground (see *pic 1*).

1

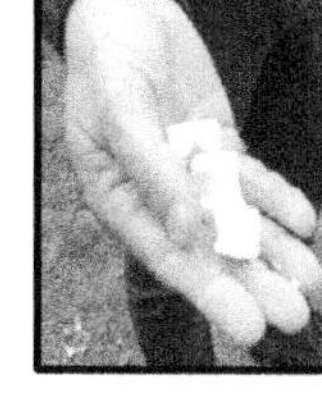

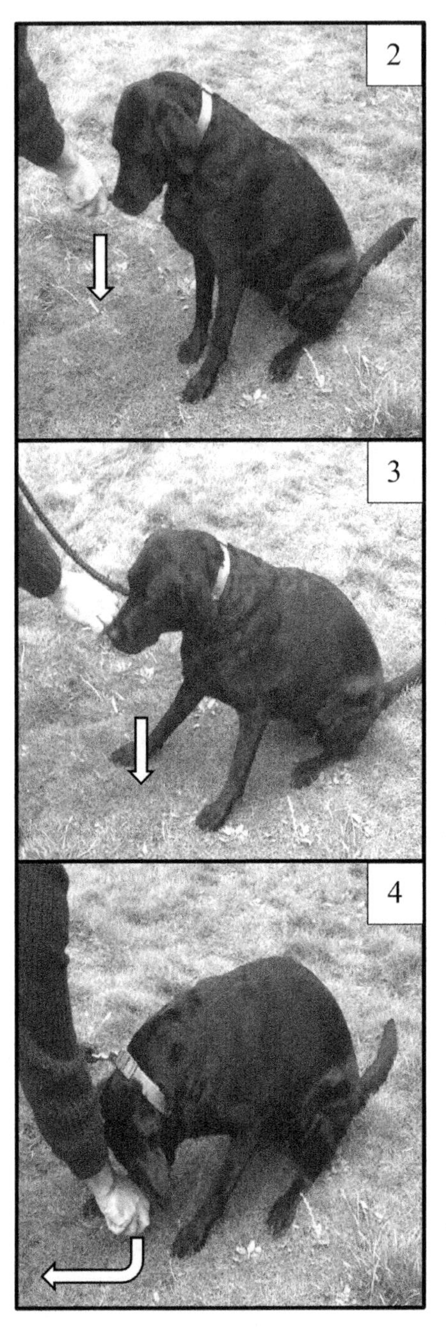

Then, say "Down" keenly, just as you move your hand towards the ground (see *pic 2*). The hand (with the treat) should end up almost in between her front paws. Placement is key—if you position the lure too far out in front of Sally, she's very likely to get up from her 'Sit' and move towards the treat and you will have to start over again. Aim to place your hand just in front of her paws (see *pic 3*). Once you've moved your hand (with the treat) towards the ground, Sally's nose will naturally move down to meet it. She should still be in a 'Sit' at this point and her back will be arched as she investigates your hand (see *pic 4*). As soon as her nose is almost touching your treat hand, slowly pull it in a straight line along the ground directly towards you and Sally should stretch out and forward, *following* the scent of the lure. Her chest and tummy should quickly touch the ground, achieving a 'Down,' (see *pic 5*) which you should reward by releasing the treat *straight away,* accompanied by a delighted "Gooood Down" and some animated body language.

<u>No pressure</u>

If Sally seems a little uneasy about assuming a 'Down' position, do encourage and motivate her but if she's persistently unsure about the activity, stop practising the exercise. Simply put training this behaviour to one side for a few days and, during this time, when she's in the 'Down' position of her own accord—naturally laying down and resting in her bed at home, for example—move towards her and make the 'Down' hand signal in front of her. Give some affection or an occasional food treat to motivate learning. You're engaging in mild conditioning here, making a positive association with the word and hand signal, keen to convey that 1) 'Down' equals 'tummy on floor' and 2) good things follow. After a few days, revert to your previous training strategy and you should be able to persuade Sally into the 'Down' position more easily than before.

Laying 'Down' but getting up again

Sometimes a dog will lay down on command but then pop straight up again—by sitting up or standing—very quickly, thinking, 'well, I've done it' and immediately look for a reward or praise. Be sensible here and avoid promoting a behaviour that isn't steady and maintained, even if your trainee did go 'Down' for a very short time. If you have a dog that does the 'laying down for a very short time before quickly sitting or standing up' behaviour, then ask your trainee to go "Down" and then quickly say "Good boy" and "Stay" just as his tummy touches the floor. Keep the hand with the lure on the ground for a few seconds or more, maintaining the 'Down' behaviour for longer, before releasing the reward and giving enthusiastic praise. After a few of these practice sessions, where your trainee is consistently being asked to lay 'Down' and 'Stay,' he will learn to lay down and to *remain in that position* before being rewarded.

The Bridge

The 'Bridge' game is one you could try at home too. This is a very useful strategy to use if your trainee is not very keen on the 'Down' initially or if you just want to try a different approach. Start by sitting on the floor with Arthur. Have him sitting beside you and pull your knees up so they are close enough to make 'a bridge' that he can crawl under, and keep your feet on the floor. Choose a valued treat, ball or a toy as your lure and ask for a "Sit" and a "Watch" (see *pic 1*). Try to keep his interest levels up by saying "Nicely" a few times to let him know a prize is on offer!

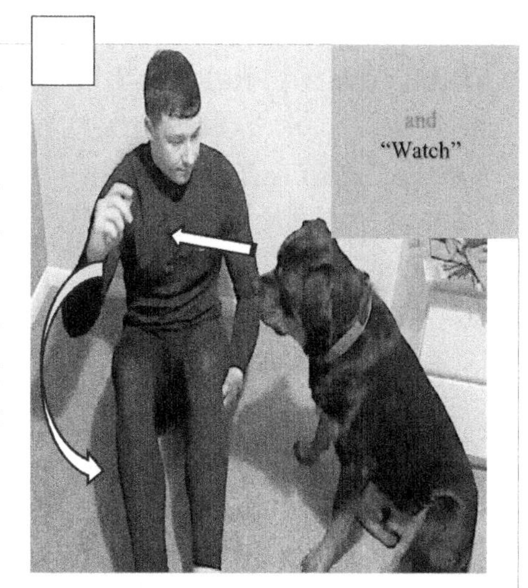

Then move your hand ...th the lure) under your ...ees towards your ...nee, saying "Nicely" ...in (see *pic 2)*. By pulling your hand back pretty SLOWLY to its starting point, lure him 'under your bridge.' Arthur will have to get 'Down' to fit under your 'bridge' *(see pic 3*) and, as he does, you can say "Down" just as he presses his

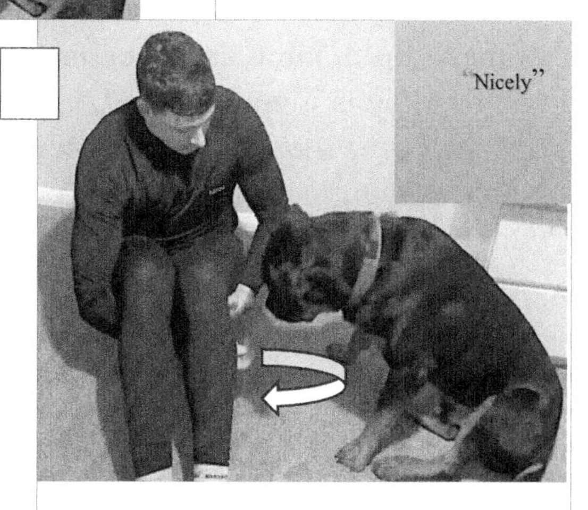

tummy on the floor to get to his reward. Release his treat *as soon as* he goes 'Down' and offer lots of upbeat praise (see *pic 4*). After teaching like this over a few days you can revisit your 'Between the paws' method of training the 'Down' command (as outlined earlier) and you should see great progress quite quickly.

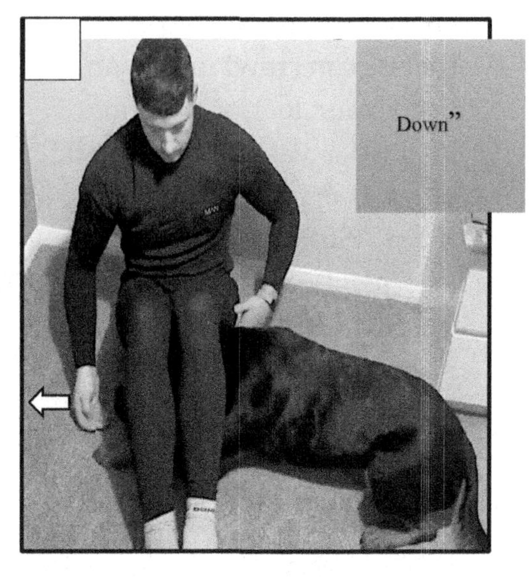

Use combinations

A few successful 'Down' exercises at any one time will be enough for most dogs in the beginning phases of training. But once your trainee is fairly proficient you can make things more interesting by adding in other commands too. A combination like 'Wait, Sit, Down, Stay, Come' can be used to make up a stimulating training game—particularly if a ball or a toy is involved—and, of course, you can build on this over time too. Practice before feeding, before a walk or before playing a game, so very positive links are made in your dog's mind with the new behaviour.

Advanced training

Once your trainee gets really good at the 'Down' command at close quarters, you can start practising it from a short distance away too. Get a few treats or another lure your trainee loves and start (in your lounge or kitchen) by positioning your trainee so he's sitting in front of you and watching you. Simply take half a step back from where you usually stand to begin the routine and teach him to go 'Down' on command from this new (short) distance, always being quick to praise any successes. If he is not being as responsive as he usually is, just go back a little bit in his direction and try again. Once you've done well a few times, stick at this distance for a few days or so, to allow your trainee to get used to the new distance/system. *Gradually* increase the distance you stand away from your trainee when giving the 'Down' command and you should get a reliable 'distance Down' before very long.

An extra pair of hands

If your trainee doesn't seem to be very keen on this new 'distance-Down' routine but is always really good when practising at close quarters, think about asking for some help from a family member or friend. Explain to your volunteer what your goal is—to get your trainee to lay down when you ask him to from a distance—and show them how you normally practice the 'Down' command when he's alongside you ... explaining where you normally stand, your visual and verbal cues and how to treat effectively. Then place a lead on your trainee and pass this to your volunteer along with a few tasty treats and ask them to practice 'Down' a few times. Once your trainee is quite happy going into a 'Down' position for your volunteer, ask them to keep hold of the lead while you say "Sit/Stay" and move a short distance away.

Then use your "Down" command enthusiastically. This time, if your trainee doesn't react to you straight away, your volunteer—standing right next to your on-lead trainee—should use the familiar verbal and visual cues to motivate your trainee to go into the 'Down.' Your volunteer is merely reinforcing the signal you are giving from a distance. If your trainee is successful, praise (from you both) should be swift to make great associations. If this type of training routine is practised frequently in short bursts, your trainee will learn quickly to listen to your distant commands as these are always being reinforced very positively at close quarters. As a result, when you practice on your own, you should see improvements in your trainee's 'Down' behaviour—when you are nearby *and* from a distance.

Chapter 30

Leave

Do not move towards

Drop or Leave

Some people use a 'Drop' command instead of 'Leave' when they want their dog to release an item he already has in his mouth. The 'Drop' behaviour can be trained by offering a trainee something he likes (a ball for example) and, once he has it in his mouth, wave another toy or juicy treat in front of his nose just as you extend your hand and say, "Drop." Once he drops the ball/toy, treat this behaviour immediately and then give him the original toy to play with again. If you do this regularly using an upbeat and playful manner, most trainees understand the 'Drop' idea very quickly. In the following pages, rather than focusing on asking your dog to drop an item he already has, we will focus on training the 'Leave' behaviour so you can ask your trainee to give space to (i.e., not move towards) certain people, other dogs, a toy or maybe something unsavoury on the ground.

Before you begin training

It would be great if your dog, Seamus, already knew the 'Stay' and 'Watch' commands before learning the 'Leave,' as these can be used effectively when training a sound 'leaving' behaviour. Also, given that you are going to be conditioning Seamus *NOT to move towards* a food treat or a toy, it makes sense to use a low or medium value lure initially, so Seamus stands a chance of being able to leave the item(s) alone. If you start by placing Seamus's favourite toy or extra special treats on the ground and then expect immediate 'leaving' success ... you will probably have put too much temptation in his way. Begin by using low or medium value treats or toys and work up from there, once you've had a number of successes.

Starting to train

While on-lead, ask Seamus to lay "Down" and to "Stay" (or "Sit and Stay" is fine too) and show him that you have a few treats or other incentives in your hand. Standing or kneeling beside him, ask him again to "Seamus, Stay" (see *pic 1*) As you place a few treats or toys on the floor a few feet away from him, say "Seamus, Stay" and "Leave," once again using your 'teacher voice' (see *pic 2*). Your position is very important here, being almost in between Seamus and the treats, so there's no way he can get to them if he decides to move towards them of his own accord.

If he leaves the temptation for a few seconds (by not moving out of position), bring one treat back towards his nose before quickly asking for a "Watch," i.e., to look into your eyes (see *pic 3*). If he watches you briefly, then offer the treat, saying, "Gooood Watch" and "Gooood Leave" heartily (see *pic 4).* Repeat the exercise (i.e., your 'Stay, Leave and Watch' combination) until all the treats you started with have been given to one very happy Seamus! By training in this way, you are conditioning Seamus to understand: A) 'not to move towards' on cue and B) to 'look back to you' immediately when he hears the word 'Leave' and C) to really enjoy the 'Leave' behaviour. As a result—once he gets good at the routine—if you see someone or something you want Seamus to leave alone when you are out on a walk and he's on or off-lead, you could say, "Seamus, Leave" and, as soon as he looks back to you, ask him to "Come" to you, for example.

Not 'Leaving'

When training the behaviour, should the on-lead Seamus move towards the treats or toys, quickly block his approach, saying, "Ah-Ah … Stay … Leave" in your teacher-like manner and if he's really not listening, pick all the treats/toys up. Take your time here and reposition him in a 'Sit' or 'Down.' Then start again by asking Seamus to "Stay" and "Leave" just as you place the items on the floor and begin the process of conditioning once more.

Bring it back

It's vital in the early stages of training that you bring the reward back to Seamus rather than asking him to move out of a waiting position and get it himself. This fixed canine positioning will block any expectation of 'movement towards' a treat, encouraging a relaxed mind and a steady 'Leave.' You'll need to practice this routine a number of times over a number of days and weeks until you've trained a comfortable 'waiting and leaving' state of mind. Try not to run before you can walk here and remember to place the treats a couple of feet away from your trainee initially—so he will be able to leave them—even though you might be tempted to move them much closer to him after only a few successes.

Using combinations of commands

Once you're confident that you have a very steady 'Leave,' you can make training more interesting by using a combination of commands. For example, you could start off walking Seamus on-lead and ask him to, "Close, Wait, Sit, Watch, Stay," before placing a few tasty treats on the ground just as you say "Leave." If he leaves the temptation alone for a short time—a few seconds or so initially—reward him by bringing the treats *to* him, verbally praise him using your "Gooood Leave" and then move on to another walking exercise or an off-lead game. Gradually extend the amount of 'Leave' time you ask for (up to about 20 seconds or so) when it's clear that he understands the game.

Leaving something while moving

Once you've taught Seamus to leave food treats or toys on the floor while he is stationary, then you can start to ask for the same 'leaving' behaviour in other situations too. With Seamus on-lead, place a ball or favourite toy on the ground while saying "Leave." Walk past the article with your trainee, asking him to "Leave" again as you approach the temptation. Use a clear 'Ah-Ah' sound if he moves towards it and use your 'Leave' command once more. Once he's left the item a couple of times, bring it to him and say "Seamus, Watch" and, if he holds his gaze on you for a few seconds, give him the reward and praise excitedly. Then maybe play a game or give him some off-lead time before beginning again. In this way, Seamus will get the idea that if he listens to you when you say "Leave," good times follow.

Leaving people and dogs

Provided you're getting a very consistent 'Leave' with treats and toys at home, then start applying this command to leaving people and dogs when outside the home too. If possible, ask for some help from a friend and their well-behaved dog while inventing a role-play where you both pass by each other in the park with your trainees on-lead. As you move closer to your volunteer, instruct Seamus to "Leave" in the usual way and, if he's obviously trying to avoid contact and is clearly not 'moving towards,' immediately reward him with a "Gooood Leave." Using your 'Watch' command alongside an enticing lure (toy or treat) is a great idea, presenting the lure just as you pass by your volunteer and their dog. This exercise will be much easier to practice successfully if your volunteer's dog is also leaving Seamus alone and paying him little attention, so choose your helper and their (level-headed) canine companion wisely. If they 'Leave' each other on command, give them the toy/ball/treat and practice this a few times. A great reward might be to let them both off-lead for some playtime.

Having trained the 'Leave' command thoroughly using toys and treats, it's important to think about your own reaction too if, for example, you see Seamus eating something nasty when he's off-lead in the park. If you find yourself in this situation, try not to shout "Seamus, Nooo! ... get away from that, you silly dog. What are you doing? No! Yuck! Baaaad dog!" Instead, jump straight into teacher mode and say, "Seamus, Leave!" and "Seamus, Come" in a matter-of-fact and upbeat tone of voice and think about using your whistle here too. How you behave is very likely to influence your trainee's reaction, so staying green and quickly finding your positive teacher mindset is very important.

Chapter 31

This Way

Follow my direction

*Search for **LoveK9 TV** on YouTube*
*to view our **This Way** video*

While walking your dog on-lead outdoors, you'll often be turning left and right when crossing the street etc., so it would be great to have a word in your command repertoire that signals to your trainee when you're about to change direction. Your focus here should be on conditioning your dog to expect a change in direction straight after he hears your 'This Way' instruction.

<u>Cue, then change direction</u>

Begin by walking your dog, Kitty, outside. Moving forward with your on-lead trainee, give the command just before you change direction, keeping her on the same side of you as you move. You could say "Kitty, This way" enthusiastically just before you begin to turn right or left, and

cue Kitty again just before you turn in a horseshoe fashion back in the direction you came from. Holding one of your trainee's treats or toys in your hand just in front of Kitty's nose will help you lure her in the direction you choose. Select a lure that will be interesting, but not one that will get your trainee too stimulated or it might work against you. Simply walk forward and place your hand (with the lure) in front of your on-lead trainee and, having given the verbal 'This way' cue, turn in a new direction and lure her by moving your hand around appropriately. If your dog is on your left-hand side then it's best to lure using your right hand (crossing over your body). If your trainee is on your right-hand side then use your left arm/hand (crossing over your body) to lure her around. Reward Kitty quickly when she's clearly listening to your cue and following your direction change. Any treats or other lures can be phased out later on or used only occasionally once Kitty has the idea, so she doesn't expect them every time you practice. Praise instead using an upbeat tone of voice with lots of 'This Way … Gooood!'

Use 'This way' when off-lead too

If you're out in the woods or park walking Kitty off-lead and you decide to change direction, it's useful to be able to signal to your trainee that you are about to take an alternative route. Using this command, there's no need to call Kitty to you; simply say, "Kitty, This way" once and move off in a particular direction. If you do this automatically every time you change direction, most dogs learn and respond quickly to 'This way' as, from their perspective, their teacher is about to take a new and potentially more exciting route.

Most trainees get to grips with the 'This Way' command in a very short time—it presents great benefits so is certainly a behaviour worth teaching and practising.

Chapter 32

Stand

Stand still

The 'Stand' command is one to train early on if you want your trainee to be handled by your vet with minimal fuss, if you want him to settle and have a green mind while grooming or if you're thinking about showing your dog. 'Stand' is also very useful when washing or drying your trainee or when you want to examine his paws or clip his nails, so it really is a valuable behaviour to teach.

Use a lure to change position

An easy way to teach your dog, Mia, to 'Stand' is to begin by asking her to "Sit." Once she's in the 'Sit' position, while holding a treat or lure in one hand, give the verbal 'Stand' instruction. At the same time, tease or lure her forward into a standing position by placing the treat or toy just in front of her nose.

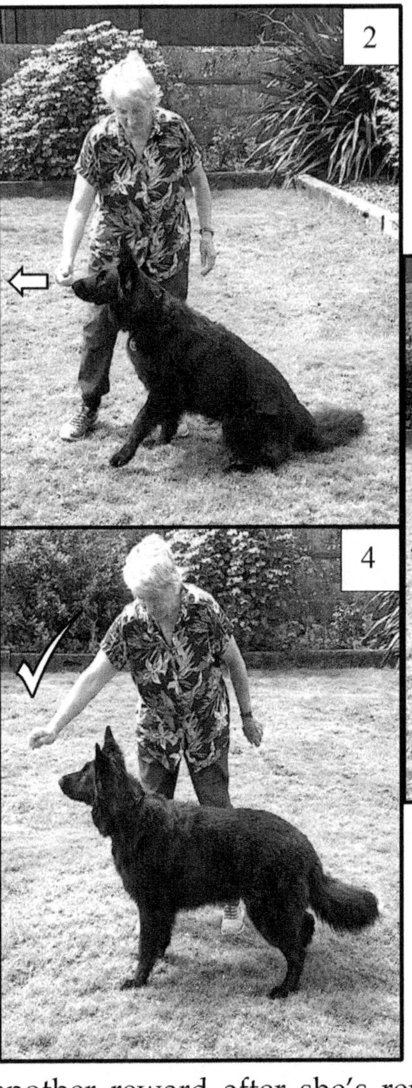

Then move it forward in a direct line away from her, so her nose (and body) changes position and she 'stands up' to get to the treat/toy.

Once Mia has moved into the correct 'Stand' position, give her the toy/treat immediately and ask her to "Stay" in that position for a few seconds, giving her another reward after she's remained standing for a short time. Some positive verbal/physical feedback and facial expressions will really help reinforce the message that she's behaving very well, so Mia is very likely to want to play the 'Stand' game again!

Use your free hand to guide

Once in a 'Stand' position, a good idea is to place your free hand—the one not holding the treat/toy—gently under your trainee's tummy to help maintain a steady 'Stand.'

Alternatively, if you place the back of your (free) hand very gently against your dog's inside back leg when he's already in the 'Stand,' he's more likely to relax and hold the position.

Practice with others

Routinely play the 'Stand, Stay' game with visitors and family members at home, asking them to run their hands over your dog—while you present a juicy treat or toy in front of him—and sometimes ask others to complete a short mock examination by taking on the role of a show judge or vet. Once completed, give the treat or play with the toy for a short time. If you practice your 'Stand' routine (preferably after a little exercise) with an upbeat vibe and a few tasty treats or a valued toy, your trainee will understand what's required in no time at all. You will then be able to use this cue effectively when checking his coat at home or when visiting your vet. It will also prove extremely useful if you intend showing your dog.

PROBLEMS and SOLUTIONS

Introduction

While some solutions to behavioural issues are explored in this section, we need to screw on our common-sense heads here. We must recognise that dogs are individuals, as are owners, families and their environments, so coming up with 'one formula for all' when attempting to change behaviour is impossible to devise. In order to modify behaviour, try to tailor the methods outlined to your own individual trainee, deviating a little here and there at times within any particular strategy to accommodate your trainee's needs. If you feel you might benefit from some practical support, then seeking some one-to-one professional advice early on is a very sensible approach.

Offer direction

Before beginning to tackle any specific behavioural issue, there's one simple concept to consider beforehand. When faced with a behaviour you want to change, focus on training new behaviours too instead of merely correcting an old one. For example, if a dog persistently lunges at the front door and jumps about frantically when visitors arrive, some might counter these issues by telling their dog "No" and *only* telling him "No". But it would be much fairer and more productive if a trainee was taught what you want him to do instead (of the misbehaviour). You might, for example, be able to motivate a dog to change old habits by putting his lead on at the front door, so you have a little more control and can guide him more easily. You could also use commands like 'Settle' and 'Wait' and follow this with a 'Sit' and 'Watch' alongside clear hand signals and a few high-value treats. You could also ask your trainee to 'Go to bed' or 'Go to your place' and lead him there—a blanket or bed nearby—and then say "Stay," so he remains in one position while your visitor enters the home comfortably. Maybe you could practice this new routine with family members or a friendly neighbour initially, so your trainee gets to grips with the new 'welcoming' routine.

Whatever behaviour you're determined to change, offering *direction* to your dog is a much more constructive system for him to follow than one that just says, "No." You should A) really hone in on and understand the behaviour that is proving problematic and B) consider what behaviour you'd really like to see happen in its place and C) then make a short-list of the commands you will use to achieve your goals before D) thinking about how you will motivate your trainee to learn (offering specific types of affection, treats, toys, games etc.) and, once you've considered your overall approach, E) rehearse your new routine in short bursts *over and over* until this new behavioural pattern becomes the norm, always fuelling/praising positive behaviour.

Chapter 33

Jumping Up or Lunging

The strategy outlined here is designed to counter 'jumping up' behaviour at the front door or when you meet someone when out walking, for example, and your trainee gets over excited—his front feet leaving the ground to meet and greet. This should not be confused with a different lunging pattern, where an on-lead dog jumps up or lunges at people (or other dogs) in an anxious or aggressive manner, as there are clearly other issues present here. So, assuming you have a trainee who 'jumps up or lunges' excitedly, what kind of plan can we devise to help manage and change this behaviour? The following is worth considering:

1) Think about safety
2) Use the right tool for the job
3) Train a very steady 'Sit'
4) Be aware of associations and value
5) Ask people to help teach your trainee
6) Exercise first, then train
7) Set up some role-play exercises
8) Meet a trainer or join a training group

1) Think about safety

When it comes to a trainee jumping up excitedly, we need to take stock of some of the safety issues involved, particularly when we think about how lunging amber canine minds will play out when they're around elderly people, children and other dogs. Given that 'a lunger' won't worry about who he jumps up on—most people and other dogs are probably fair game—we must try to teach our canine charges to stop the behaviour and condition positive ones in its place. This will be much easier to achieve with puppies and younger dogs rather than having to address it when a trainee increases in size, muscle and body weight. The message here is to take the behaviour seriously early on.

2) Use the right tool for the job

If your trainee is already very practiced at the whole lunging behaviour, consider changing your existing toolset, at least in the short-term. Think about using a double-ended clip lead attached to the harness alongside a wide-fitting collar, as mentioned in chapter 12 (*Close or Heel)* earlier, or maybe you prefer having your lead only attached to a wide collar. Once you have a connection to the collar area, your trainee is more likely to listen more attentively and any previous lunging habits can often be reduced more easily. Or maybe a head collar, a figure-of-8 lead or similar tool will work better for you, as these offer more control of the head area and will increase your ability to influence your trainee and manage any jumping—do some research here so you can work out what tool will really suit you and your trainee.

3) Train a very steady 'Sit'

It might seem like a very obvious point to make but if your dog is in a 'Sit' position and remains there, he won't be jumping up. Training a good 'Sit, Watch, Stay' routine can be very helpful when working against any jumping habit.

4) Be aware of associations and value

Let's imagine you have Mila, the sweetest of puppies, living at home. You're walking down the street and Mila spots your friend Trevor approaching and she gets very excited—going straight into her exuberant body-wag and over-the-top behaviour. Trevor comes over to you and, flattered by the excitement and love that Mila is clearly bestowing on him, quickly makes a fuss of her excitedly, regularly using her name. This only fuels Mila's already mid/high amber mind and her front paws don't spend too much time on the ground during the entire interaction. Mila loves the whole meeting and gets very positive feedback throughout. Trevor is obviously a kind man with sweet intentions but, by acting in this way, he's promoting the wrong colour of mind in your trainee. He gives affection when Mila jumps up, talks to her excitedly and uses her name repeatedly when her mind is in the high amber zone, reinforcing the message to Mila that 'This person obviously loves me and what I'm doing. Wow! Getting excited and presenting myself like this feels great!' Then, to top it all, a very generous Trevor reaches in his pocket for a juicy treat and gives it to a lunging Mila, so she is completely convinced this strategy is an absolute winner—one to practice for the future. As outlined previously, dogs are very good at learning by making links or associations so we should be careful about the messages we're sending.

Many trainers and behaviourists talk about 'presenting great value to great behaviour' and 'presenting little (or no) value to poor behaviour'—a concept that is very worthwhile when considering any jumping or lunging. If Mila doesn't get lots of positive feedback when she meets people by jumping up, then she is very likely to stop or reduce that behaviour. On the other hand, if she meets and greets with all four paws on the ground and is praised heartily, then this behaviour will present great value for Mila, so this is how she is most likely to choose to behave in future.

5) Ask people to help teach your trainee

When meeting people outside you could start interactions with, "It's really lovely to see you, Trevor. Mila's in training at the moment so we need to give her something to do before we say hello. I've read that we shouldn't get her too excited when meeting," or say something like this. Give Trevor a couple of treats and ask him to encourage Mila to 'Sit' and 'Watch' him for about five seconds. If she's a good girl then Trevor could give her a couple of treats and some physical affection alongside an enthusiastic "Gooood Mila," provided she's not jumping up of course. At the end of the interaction, thank Trevor for being a great teacher and for helping with Mila's schooling—this is likely to mean he will present a more positive teacher-like vibe the next time you meet up. In this way Mila will learn how the whole 'meet and greet' system works and figure out how she can get great value/rewards.

6) Exercise first, then train

It's important to swing the likelihood of success in your favour by exercising your dog, Bear, thoroughly before engaging in any reconditioning. If his energy levels are a little drained he will be more able to listen to your guidance. Practice walking and running Bear first, on and off lead if possible, and really get into your positive teacher role by asking him to "Sit" and "Wait," etc. on occasion too. Focus on having some fun doing something he loves—chasing a ball or maybe running in the park or on the beach—actively rewarding any positive behaviour throughout. Here, you're simply ensuring Bear is listening and responding to you while having a lovely time (shedding energy) before you start training him to change any jumping habits.

7) Set up some simple role-play exercises

Once you've exercised Bear and he's a little fatigued, set up a scenario that would normally motivate him to jump up. This might involve asking a family member, neighbour or friend to visit you at home, if this is where much of the jumping behaviour takes place. If Bear usually gets very excited when meeting someone when out on a walk, ask someone to walk up to you outside your home. Try to be creative here and give some thought to where and who you could meet.

Jumping up at home, when visitors arrive

If Bear normally greets people by hurling himself exuberantly at any visitor to your home, front feet in mid-air to say "Hello," then a good starting point would be to invite a family member or friend around to your home so Bear can practice a different approach. You, of course, must get yourself into a calm 'teacher mode' frame of mind and have mentally rehearsed what you would like to see happen. Will Bear 'Sit' and 'Wait' and then go to 'Bed' beside the front door or how will the story unfold? How do you think Bear will behave? What exactly do you want him to do at different times? What commands will you use throughout? Ask yourself, 'What will I do if Bear starts to get really excited? … how will I behave? … what colour will I (try to) be? … what vibe will I pass to my trainee?' If you are very clear about what to expect and what you want to happen, your guidance will be too, so Bear is likely to learn the new routine very quickly.

Your (carefully chosen) volunteer should be given clear instructions on how they can help—don't just assume they will know how to behave or understand when they should reward. You'll need to tell them about the colour system and what you are trying to achieve, so you will need to spell things out to help your volunteer feel confident and be really consistent and effective when teaching Bear. A nice cup of tea and some cake might be a fair exchange? Sharing information like, "When you come in, if Bear is behaving like a loon, you must do this and behave like ..." and "When we go into the lounge, I will sit here and you will …" etc. will be very helpful guidance. Also, invest a little time explaining how important it is not to present any value to any unwelcome jumping behaviour, even if Bear looks very cute at times. It's also vital to explain about promoting good behaviour by presenting value at the right time, so Bear will learn positive habits quickly.

A good approach might be to ask your friend, Eve, to ignore the on-lead Bear—don't look at or talk to him—as she enters the home, particularly if his colour is anything other than green or low amber or if he's jumping up. Eve should let you get on with managing Bear as she enters and focus her attention on interacting with you rather than an exuberant trainee. Eve can give brief affection to Bear—when all paws are on the floor—but she should try not to make him the centre of attention. Remind Eve that she's going to give him lots of affection, but in a couple of minutes or so, when Bear's colour and vibe are more appropriate. Invite Eve into the kitchen or lounge and, keeping Bear on-lead, ask her to take a seat while you sit down too with Bear alongside. You, of course, can use your 'Settle,' 'Wait' and 'Sit,' commands at times and, after a few minutes have passed and Bear is wearing a green or low amber mind, then you can let the lead go or take it off him so he can say hello to your friend. If he gets too exuberant at any time, Eve needs to withdraw affection—value—and give the 'Settle' command while you regain some control by putting Bear back on-lead, etc. After a short time, ask Eve to leave the home again and to return in a few minutes to restart the exercise.

After a few mock visits, Bear is likely to get the hang of things and behave more reasonably, at which point Eve can greet him a little sooner than before. If he is behaving well and in a good colour, suggest to Eve that she asks Bear to "Sit" and "Watch," etc. just as she comes in, giving him a few timely food rewards—these will promote Bear's positive mindset and make great associations for the future. He will learn which behaviour and colour gets rewarded and which offers little value, so he's likely to present a more positive vibe when your next visitor arrives. You will need to practice your new routine at home many times—with a few different volunteers—before you'll see very positive changes in Bear's behaviour; but this effort on your part will be time very well spent.

Jumping up outside, when meeting and greeting

If Bear is usually a jumper/lunger when seeing or meeting people outside on a walk, then a good idea might be to involve another friend, Gayle, to help teach Bear how he should behave. The approach here is much the same as before—both you and Gayle are going to present value when you see welcome behaviour and deliberately withdraw any if you see excited jumping behaviour. 'Value' could be attention, verbal and physical affection, a toy, a game or a food reward. You'll need to think about what lead or other accessory you will use to walk Bear and remember to have a few very tasty treats and maybe his favourite toy in your pocket to help distract and motivate. Give Gayle a few special treats too, which she can use when interacting with Bear at times.

Arrange to meet Gayle outside on a walk and explain to her how she should behave during the interaction. She should approach you and Bear confidently and, initially, stop and speak only to you—not Bear—for a short time. By not giving Bear too much attention or affection when he is in the wrong colour, Gayle will help to control the situation and motivate Bear to go into a more reasonable colour before she presents any value. You can practice your 'Sit, Wait, Settle and Watch' commands and suggest to Gayle that she does the same when engaging with Bear. After your brief meeting, say "Goodbye" to Gayle and continue on your walk for a few minutes. Then meet up with her again, so Bear practices the routine and learns what is welcome and unwelcome behaviour. Both of you can and should reward Bear's positive vibe, colour and behaviour whenever you see it.

Once you've built up a good level of confidence and control in quieter practice areas with different people over a few weeks, then think about taking Bear to places where introductions are likely to occur 'for real'—to a village or park, for example—where you can meet other people and their dogs. Walking with friends or family members is a good idea too, at least initially, so they can offer you some support while you teach Bear how to behave well.

8) Meet a trainer or join a training group

If you're still having some jumping problems and feel like you need a little support, think about contacting a trainer or behaviourist and arrange to meet up on a one-to-one basis. Also, consider joining a dog training group to help teach your trainee how to behave well through a series of common exercises, like walking past people and their dogs at close quarters.

Chapter 34

Separation Anxiety

Why is it that some dogs can be completely fine when left at home and others go into panic mode? Research is not very conclusive here but suggests that many dogs, given their very strong attachment to humans, find it difficult to automatically know that 'being left behind' and 'being apart' is a normal and reasonable event. Our dogs need to be taught that this 'being left behind' behaviour at home is 'okay,' so it's preferable to do this conditioning when a dog is quite young, rather than waiting until a trainee develops an anxious behaviour which then has to be overcome. Some professionals now call this type of anxiety 'separation distress,' given that certain dogs can become very destructive, bark incessantly, pace repeatedly, get sick and maybe urinate or poop in the home if left for any period of time. It's important to outline that any dog behaving like this is not being naughty—they are worried and stressed as they are not with their human—so we need to be very fair and kind when educating them.

There are many dynamics here. Each dog with this condition is likely to have very different life experiences to others. Some will be younger trainees, others much older, some might be rescue dogs, some will have mild anxiety and others severe and people and home environments will be very different too, so it's impossible to present one strategy that will instantly help all dogs. With this in mind, applying lots of good common sense is very important. Tailor the following strategy to your individual dog and your own situation and focus on your goal—teaching your trainee that being 'left behind at home' is not something to worry about.

So, whether you already have a trainee that gets quite stressed whenever you leave home or maybe you have a puppy or rescue dog that needs to learn about 'staying green' when being left for the first time, let's explore a strategy we can use to help.

1. Basic instincts
2. Limit access
3. Limit space
4. Prepare the resting area
5. Use Kongs
6. Play some background music/sound
7. Exercise him, then leave him
8. Leave, but stay at home with your trainee
9. Pay attention to how you return
10. Leave the home
11. Use a visual soother
12. Dog Appeasing Pheromones (D.A.P.)
13. Use a Thunder Shirt
14. Investigate Rescue Remedies
15. Having another dog at home
16. Seek professional advice

1) Basic instincts

Science tells us that dogs are probably the only creatures to have domesticated themselves. They began living with humans well before the dawn of agriculture, so their inbuilt attachment and drive or *need* to be with people should not be underestimated. So, when we think about leaving a healthy trainee behind at home, we should appreciate that it might not sit very well with his inner make up and he's likely to get worried and worked up. Therefore, it's our responsibility to teach him there will be times when he will 'stay behind at home' and do our very best to educate our trainee to be okay with this. So, how can we start teaching and conditioning?

2) Limit access

A subtle, but often effective, strategy to start conditioning your trainee to remain in a reasonable colour when being left behind is to put up a couple of baby-gates at home, one at the entrance to the kitchen and another to the lounge, for example. This is a short-term strategy designed to teach your trainee that he doesn't always have access to you when you're at home, even though he can still see and/or hear you. When you go into the kitchen, close the baby-gate behind you for very short time periods, leaving your trainee on the other side. Continue doing what you're doing and return without saying very much at all. As days roll into weeks, *gradually* extend the amount of time you are 'away' from your trainee indoors and he should begin to get the idea that, while he can't be with you, nothing negative ever takes place and you always come back fairly quickly. In this way, he should get much better at 'not having access to you' over time. This is a very good starting point to leaving him behind at home.

3) Limit space

When leaving their trainee at home, some very well-intentioned owners might let him roam around freely—giving him access to many rooms when he's at home—the perception being that he'll be more comfortable in a spacious environment. This is, however, a human perspective and can often add insecurities rather than make an anxious dog feel more comfortable. Ideally, your trainee should have 'a place to call his own' when being left at home—a bed in a kitchen or utility room would be a suitable space, replicating a cosy den which, in time, he'll associate with settling down and feeling safe. This smaller area will encourage him to relax and be quiet, rather than potentially spending his time roaming around the home looking for you, only ending up getting increasingly stressed while you're out. Where will your dog's resting area be?

4) Prepare the resting area

Making your trainee's resting area very inviting seems like a basic point to make, but it's a worthy strategy when motivating him to want to remain in a positive state when you leave. Give him access to fresh drinking water and focus on making his bed/environment very comfortable. Leaving a few of his favourite toys in his resting area should provide some interest too and should help occupy and distract your trainee. Vigorously rub your hands on an old towel and use this as part of the bedding as well, as this will remind him of some familiar human scent and he's likely to achieve a more relaxed resting state.

5) Use Kongs

One training accessory you could use here is a Kong. This is a cone-shaped hard plastic toy, hollow in the middle, designed to be stuffed with some juicy morsels that will help occupy your dog when you're not around. The idea is that you stuff the item full of enticing goodies and your trainee will spend ages trying to get these out, rather than focusing on the fact that you're not there. The choice of juicy morsels is important and time invested here is well spent. Finely sliced meat such as cooked chicken or liver cake, cheese and some of your dog's kibble/biscuits can all be used but you'll know best what gets your trainee's interest, so you choose. Smearing a little organic peanut butter on the inside wall of the Kong will also add value here. Having placed your concoction of food inside the Kong, put some bread or something bulky in at the very end to lock everything in. Your dog will have to figure out how to extract the treats that he'll definitely smell, so energy will be sapped and his mind will be distracted in this way.

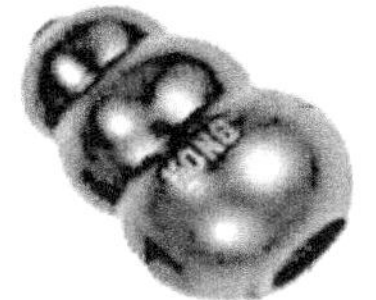

If you decide to purchase a Kong, look at the manufacturer's descriptions to figure out the best size to get for your trainee. Get him used to investigating a Kong laden with treats while you're at home over a few days and regularly give him some of his usual food in the Kong at feeding time, rather than only using it when you leave him, otherwise it will be associated only with 'leaving him,' which is not what you want. Give the filled Kong to your trainee in his resting area too at times to build up his confidence in and familiarity with the new system.

If you're going to leave more than one dog in an enclosed area then it's sensible to avoid using Kongs altogether, even if the dogs get on very well around food when you're at home. The danger here is that Kongs might end up as a focal point of dispute and fuel confrontations, rather than help you achieve your goal of 'rest and relaxation' while you're in a different room or away from home for a short time.

In addition to a Kong some people use a LickiMat (where you could smear a favourite paste or something similar into the grooves) to help engage a trainee and reduce anxiety levels through distraction, so you may want to look these up online or ask at your local pet shop.

6) Play some background music/sound

Another useful tip when motivating a canine mind to settle is to have some sounds playing in the room where your trainee's going to be left. A radio playing on a medium-volume setting will soothe most dogs and give the illusion of company, as will a ticking clock positioned near your dog's bed. Separation anxiety recordings are available on YouTube and elsewhere, providing easy access to sounds that have been carefully selected to help dogs relax at home—do a little research here and select something you think might be suitable.

7) Exercise him, then leave him

Walking your dog and really working him using a game like 'Fetch' before you leave him at home will help swing the likelihood of success in your favour too. Any dog that's already burnt off some energy is probably going to be able to cope a little better with being left on his own for a short while. Remember, exercise him first and then practice your leaving routine.

8) Leave, but stay at home with your trainee

Once you've prepared the environment and exercised your trainee, you are ready to start conditioning. Practice leaving your trainee, Maggie, behind in 'her area' for very short time periods when you are at home and want to make a cup of tea, for example. Gradually extend the amount of time you are away ... from one minute one day to two the next and build this up gradually. Practice a couple of times a day (or more) over a few weeks, so she can build up her confidence levels. If you see any negative colour appear at any time, try to stick to 'being away' for slightly shorter time periods (which she can handle) and do this for a couple of days, so Maggie can acclimatise to the process without getting stressed.

A good approach to 'leaving Maggie' might be to calmly invite her into her resting area using an upbeat and welcoming tone. Ask Maggie to go to her bed using your casual and familiar, "Maggie, Come … This way … Bed … Gooood girl" routine. Avoid too much talking at this stage, except to give the odd command and quiet praise, trying to steer clear of phrases like, 'I won't be long, Maggie darling, everything will be okay. Love you,' etc., however well-intentioned your words might be. Focus on getting your trainee to hone in on the goodies being provided—the Kong, the chew toy or a few treats, for example. If you're confident when departing, this is the feeling that you'll pass to your trainee as you leave. If you're turning around and frequently talking to her, Maggie might get conflicting information—you're leaving her but you're speaking to her and looking at her, suggesting that you want her to engage with you. It's far better to use positive matter-of-fact body language and simply say, "Won't be long" or "Stay there, darling" or "Settle" or something like this. Then turn away and leave her … just go and make your cup of tea. The message and vibe you're passing on here is that you know exactly what you're doing—Maggie has no need to worry … you're just practising the familiar 'leaving and coming back' routine.

If you have to go into her room/area to reassure her, then remain green, settle her down calmly and ask for a green-ish mind before leaving her again with a simple 'Stay/Settle' or 'Won't be long' phrase alongside a confident and content (rather than a very emotional) vibe.

9) Pay attention to how you return

Once you've conditioned a certain level of relaxation and Maggie's been quiet for a very short period of time, go back to her, quietly and confidently. Remain pretty low-key at this stage as you want to convey the message that this leaving and coming back routine is really 'no big deal.' If you come back and give Maggie lots of excited praise and attention immediately, your behaviour might be interpreted as: 'Well done for getting through it!' which will work against you when you next leave. Once you're happy Maggie is acting reasonably, give her lots of gentle and quiet affection. Repeat the exercise over and over each day, *very* gradually varying and extending the 'leaving' periods until she's happy being left for short sessions. All the time, you are conditioning Maggie to know what's expected and, before long, you should see a relaxed girl at home, very familiar with the whole 'leaving' routine.

10) Leave the home

After a few weeks conditioning Maggie to be left 'in her area' while you are in another area/room at home—provided she's quite good at it—you're ready to rehearse leaving her behind at home while you go outside. Use all the tools at your disposal to tip the likelihood of success in your favour—exercise Maggie beforehand, introduce a Kong 'full of goodies' and/or a safe chew toy, have some soothing music playing, use a ticking clock and make her bed very comfortable. Think for a few minutes about 'how you want things to go' before you actually take Maggie to her resting area, picturing what will happen. You'll go to the area where her bed is and then what? Take a little time to play out the next set of events in your mind and then 'go for it' in a controlled and calm manner. This routine is much the same as before but this time your trainee may realise that you have left the home so, at least in the very beginning, it's important to keep practice sessions *very* brief. You are looking for short 'successes' to build on, so this should be your goal. Try to practice a few times a day and build up the time you 'go outside and return' from one minute to two and then ten or fifteen minutes after a week or so (depending on how your trainee is doing). As before, if you can detect that Maggie is a little stressed one day, reduce the time you are 'away' for the next few days until she's comfortable at this level and then gradually work up again from there. Manage your emotions when you return to Maggie—do share affection of course, but take note of the colours in front of you and 'be the teacher' here. If you are consistent in training Maggie should be quite happy to be left behind at home for longer periods in the future.

11) Use a visual soother

There is an older method of conditioning that can help some dogs when being left behind at home, one certainly worth integrating into your overall strategy. Choose an object such as a mug—something robust that wouldn't ordinarily interest Leisel, your juvenile trainee. This item will act as her visual soother. Place the item on a shelf or on a windowsill—out of reach, but somewhere Leisel can clearly see it—and sit down for a minute or so at home. Whenever the visual soother is used and in position, you must remember not to interact with Leisel at all—don't make eye or body contact and try not to speak to her either during this time. After a couple of minutes or so, go straight to the item and *place it back* in its usual position, making sure she sees you moving it. If her mind is in a positive colour after you've moved the mug then interact with her verbally with a "Come ... Gooood 'Settle'..." alongside a few cuddles. Over a few days you can extend the amount of time the 'no interaction' item/game is in place to 5 minutes or more ... practice this in short'ish bursts so she'll get the idea that A) 'mug in position' means 'no interaction from you' for a short time and B) all is very well.

After a few days, provided you know your trainee seems to be getting the gist, you can start using the mug to develop things a little further. This time, put your visual cue in 'its place'—where Leisel can see it—and leave her behind a baby-gate while you go to another area of the home, returning very soon afterwards to replace the mug and share affection with Leisel. Once you've seen regular 'out of sight' successes you can extend the time you're away *very gradually* and work up to being able to go upstairs and make a bed or take a shower, for example. Over a short period of time, Leisel should grow in confidence and eventually make the 'no interaction' and 'all is well' associations with the familiar item. As time progresses and you begin to practice leaving Leisel at home, she's likely to make the association between 'seeing the mug' and registering that 'you'll come back and move it'—returning it to its usual position. Some dogs relax more as a result of this 'visual soother' idea, so do try it.

12) Dog Appeasing Pheromones (D.A.P.)

When a puppy nurses from his mother, pheromones are released to help generate and maintain a settled juvenile mind during the feeding process. Manufactured DAPs mimic these natural pheromones so we should be open to trying these products to see if they eliminate or reduce stress in dogs we're leaving behind at home.

You can buy DAPs from your vet, pet shop or online. The product can be bought in a spray form, a plug-in dispenser and a wearable collar. If you're specifically interested in using a DAP to counter separation anxiety, given that you already know your trainee will be staying behind in a fairly small area, the plug-in dispenser might be a good choice. Follow manufacturer guidelines here, but plug it in near your dog's bed well before you think about leaving him.

13) Use a Thunder Shirt

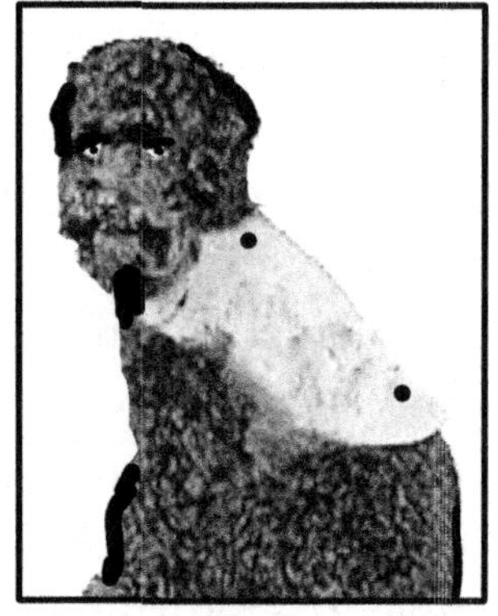

Thunder shirts or thunder jackets are body wraps that apply gentle and constant pressure around a dog's body. It's a bit like you or I wearing a t-shirt that's two sizes too small—these 'wraps' can have a dramatic calming effect for some fearful dogs, almost keeping them in constant cuddle-mode while making some comforting contact with key areas of the body. You will need to invest a little time getting your trainee acclimatised to this garment, so don't give up on the concept when you put it on him initially as he might have an expression that reads, 'What the hell?!' It's really important to get him used to wearing it at different times of the day and use it out on walks too on occasion—your goal is to make it a very familiar item, one that he should grow to love wearing. Manufacturers claim good product success rates re: helping with issues like fear of thunder, fear of fireworks, separation anxiety and others, so thunder shirts are definitely worth considering as part of the solution here.

14) Investigate Rescue Remedies

Some people regularly use a rescue remedy to help with separation anxiety as manufacturers claim this can work wonders for some animals that are impatient, fearful, have been through a traumatic event or have a fear of thunder or fireworks. You simply mix in a few drops of the (often homeopathic) remedy with food daily and this can help some dogs achieve a reasonable state of mind while you are not at home. This remedy, of course, should be used alongside other strategies outlined here rather than on its own. Do consider using a pet rescue remedy—it may prove a valuable addition to your wider 'leaving the home' strategy. Find out more by searching for 'pet rescue remedy' online or ask at your local pet shop and do some research on homeopathic remedies like Aconite and Valerian.

15) Having another dog at home

Some people feel that the company of another dog at home might be an obvious solution here and may consider getting a companion for their trainee, in an attempt to counter separation distress. Another dog at home may present great comfort for *some* dogs but this is not always the case. It sounds pretty logical, initially at least, that if a dog has another 'buddy' at home, any anxiety will be reduced when being left behind indoors. Research, however, suggests that dogs tend to put 'being with humans' into a different mental category to 'being with dogs' and, given that a dog's separation distress is born from 'missing their humans,' the presence of another dog (even if he's very confident and happy to be left at home) is not guaranteed to present major benefits.

You could try experimenting here by asking a friend if they will let you 'borrow' their (calm) dog—your trainee and this dog should know each other very well and always get along famously, of course—to investigate if your trainee is more settled when being left at home (for short periods) with another (calm) canine presence or not. Please remember to always exercise dogs very well before practising leaving them together at home. Technology can help here too, so think about capturing some video footage of the pair indoors to help confirm or reject the notion that having another (balanced) dog at home is likely to improve your trainee's lot.

16) <u>Seek professional advice</u>

If you have a dog that gets almost panic-stricken and becomes *extremely* stressed every time you even think about leaving home and you're genuinely concerned about his overall health and wellbeing, consider speaking with an experienced dog trainer or behaviourist—someone who has helped treat this condition effectively previously—so you can get some practical one-to-one support tailored to your individual dog, situation and home environment.

Also, consider making an appointment to see your vet—they will be able to establish if your dog is fit and healthy, rule out any underlying medical factors and offer key professional advice. They can also tell you about any products—medical and herbal—that are available that might help relax your dog and address any 'episodes of extreme stress' whenever possible.

If you use this approach to 'leaving your trainee' and are very consistent and positive when teaching your routine, your dog will learn that being left behind is very short-term, nothing bad ever happens and you always come back. Start slowly and in time you should have a relaxed mind waiting for you at home.

Chapter 35

Getting Very Excited in the Car

Having a dog moving around freely and excitedly inside any vehicle is obviously very dangerous and likely to prove very stressful for all. Your focus around 'car training' should be on keeping your trainee's level of excitement as low as possible all of the time, starting well before you even contemplate inviting him into the car. Let's explore one strategy you could use to help get your trainee into a reasonable state of mind when travelling:

1) Travelling safely
2) Recognise triggers
3) Plan ahead
4) Ask for a calm and collected vibe
5) Use your commands effectively
6) Invite your trainee into the car
7) Take your time
8) Go on short journeys initially
9) Increase your journey times
10) Support

1) <u>Travelling safely</u>

Highway Codes tell us we should make sure dogs and other animals are suitably restrained when in a vehicle, so they cannot distract us while driving or injure us (or themselves) if the vehicle stops quickly. Asking your dog to go into a crate when travelling in the car can be an ideal solution for some—a crate must be properly secured so it can't move around. Covering the top of it with a blanket or rug (think of a curtain pelmet) will help block some potential triggers when travelling, providing a means of having a quieter and safer journey for all involved. Even if you're not too keen on using crates, you could consider them if you're having difficulty managing your dog's excitement levels when driving. Alternatively, some people invest in purpose-built cages and guards fitted inside their vehicle, which are a great idea to help keep you and your dog safe and comfortable while travelling. Others use a simple dog harness and seat-belt clip to ensure their trainee 'belts up' when on the move.

What will work best for you and your dog?

2) Recognise triggers

Firstly, recognise that any excitement usually starts with a trigger or multiple triggers. It may well be that your trainee starts to act up when you get his lead or pick up your car keys, or just as he sees or enters the car. Another likely source of excitement is when the engine is turned on or, very often, a dog gets more heightened by a combination of these factors. Identify when and where your trainee's triggers occur, observe his colours and note them mentally for the future so when you practice again you'll be able to 'get in quickly' with commands like 'Wait' and 'Settle.'

3) Plan ahead

As mentioned in previous sections, try to exercise your trainee before you try to condition any new behaviour—if he's a little fatigued he will be able to modify his familiar heightened behaviour more easily. Also, think about using a thunder shirt as part of this experience too as, sometimes, wearing this garment/tool can help keep your trainee's mind in a more reasonable colour.

Leave the home in your usual teacher-like manner by getting your trainee settled indoors, calling him to you, putting on his lead, praising him quietly and asking him to listen to you well before you depart. Try to keep a lid on any over-excitement, no matter how much you might like to see your dog looking forward to the car journey. Do this consistently by saying, "Ah-Ah" and "Settle" quickly if you need to show you're not too happy with his colour or excited behaviour at any stage. With your trainee on-lead alongside you, ask him to "Wait" as you open your front door and remain there until he's in a reasonable colour, not whining and definitely not jumping around excitedly. Praise any positive behaviour quietly so your trainee is clear about what you consider welcome behaviour. Plan ahead and allow some extra time to accommodate this patient approach of moving your trainee quietly, step by step, from the home towards the car.

4) Ask for a calm and collected vibe

Once he's reasonably settled, start to leave the home—keeping a smile in the line—and ask him to "Wait," "Sit" and "Settle" again as you get near the car. Make sure that all car doors are closed so your trainee isn't already mentally heading for an entrance. The message you're trying to send is that moving towards the car is no reason to get excited. Give verbal affection and a treat once he's settled next to the vehicle. After a very short time call the exercise off and take him out for a walk on foot or play a game with a ball in the back garden.

Repeat this routine for a few days, a number of times each day if you can, until you achieve a relaxed mind when approaching the car and then practice the same exercise while the car engine is running. The message you're sharing—the association you're making—is clear: 'proximity to the car = a green or low amber mind' and 'engine running = a relaxed mind' too.

5) Use your commands effectively

I'm sure you're already getting the idea that the overall strategy here simply breaks down the activity of your trainee 'travelling in the car' into its component parts, going right back to where the activity started … getting the keys and your lead indoors and then taking each step in turn, asking and motivating him to remain settled throughout. While it takes time and patience, try to manage any excitement at each stage by using your 'Wait,' 'Sit' and 'Settle' commands effectively—this is crucial to success. Praise any positive behaviour quickly so your trainee knows he's on the right track.

6) Invite your trainee into the car

Once he can approach and remain near the car in a fairly relaxed manner, the next phase is to then open a car door and repeat the 'Wait' exercise. Invite your (reasonably) relaxed trainee into the car by using both a verbal command and a hand gesture. If he gets excited at any stage, go back a step—ask him to leave the car immediately and give a 'Wait' command again outside. Be calm and persistent and repeat the exercise until you get the settled behaviour you're looking for inside the car. Reward any positive behaviour so you stand a fair chance of seeing this again the next time you practice.

7) Take your time

After you've accomplished the goals set out so far, try not to rush things. Behaviours can take time to recondition so please be patient or you might find you have to go back a step and start over. Practice inviting your trainee into the car and take a little time to settle him down. Then just sit in the car with the engine running for about two minutes at a time, sitting in the same seat you would if you were actually using the car to go to the park. Aim for 'small successes' initially so finish practising while your trainee is being well behaved rather than waiting for a high amber mind to show itself. You will need to practice this routine a number of times before you see good behaviour, so try to get in a few sessions each day.

8) Go on short journeys initially

Before too long—maybe after a week or two of conditioning—start going on short journeys. But, for a few days, it would be a good idea if your trainee doesn't leave the car at all when you take him out. Simply take him in the car with you but return home soon afterwards, asking him to 'Wait' in the car patiently on your return. Then open the car door and slowly invite him out and take him indoors or go for a walk on foot. This helps reinforce the notion in your trainee's mind that a car journey doesn't always present lots of value—travelling in the car doesn't always mean he'll end up having a lovely run in the park, for example. As a result, expectation and excitement levels should naturally decrease as you practice.

9) Increase your journey times

Once your confidence has grown over shorter journeys, extend the time you're out and vary your routine by going to the park sometimes and occasionally return home after a short drive. Use your commands to help instruct and guide your trainee throughout. 'Settle,' 'Watch,' 'Wait' and 'Sit' all spring to mind—these are your verbal tools, presenting opportunities to guide and make positive associations. Practice makes perfect, so try to build up a routine that you and your trainee can follow every time you're both going out in the car.

10) Support

If you use good common sense, remain patient and stick to your strategy, you should be able to drive to the park and go on safe and peaceful car journeys before very long, confident that your trainee will behave well throughout the journey. Get some support from family members too by including them in your practice sessions. If, however, you're having real trouble influencing your dog and excitement levels are just too much to handle, talking with an experienced trainer/behaviourist early in the process is definitely a great approach. They will be able to offer one-to-one practical support and show you how to change any car-related excitement levels using positive techniques.

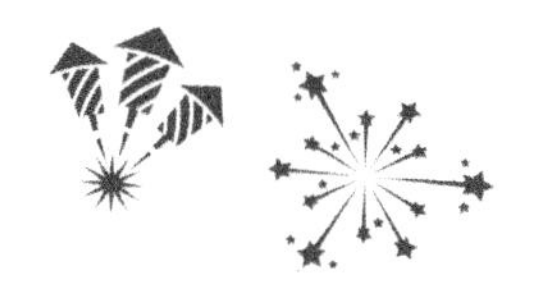

Chapter 36

Fireworks, Storms and Loud Noises

Fireworks, thunder and lightning, gunfire, sirens and bird scarers are some of the noises our dogs can find very worrying and intimidating. People who have more than one dog living at home often say that one can be absolutely fine in these situations, listening almost excitedly and watching intently while working out what and where the noise is, then simply ignoring the sound after a short time. Another dog, maybe even a littermate, might behave very differently and slink off nervously to the back of a room, behind a couch or under a bed, trying desperately to retreat and find a quiet refuge where he can lie low until 'that noise' goes away. This 'hiding away while shaking' behaviour is one of nature's ways of allowing some dogs cope with the desperately anxious situation they find themselves in, existing in almost a frozen state until the terror passes.

It can be *really* uncomfortable for an owner to have to watch a beloved canine in obvious distress when nothing much can be done to control the source of the problem. It's therefore important to know how you should behave and what you should do. Understanding what you should avoid doing in such circumstances is also a key factor in helping any trainee under stress.

Let's explore the following strategy:

1) Exercise thoroughly
2) Play things down
3) Avoid nurturing the wrong colour
4) Offer security
5) Use gentle contact to soothe
6) Be careful with aversion therapy
7) Play some recordings
8) DAPs and Thunder shirts
9) Homeopathic remedy
10) Professional advice

1) Exercise thoroughly

If you know 'that noise' is likely to happen at a particular time—fireworks on New Year's Eve, for example—exercising your dog well beforehand will drain his energy levels, so you will have a tired and more relaxed mind at home when any commotion arises.

2) Play things down

One approach you could use when you hear a noise like a firework or a clap of thunder is to try to pay it and your dog as little (obvious) attention as possible. This might appear like a passive, cold or even a 'lazy way out' but this is a strategy worth knowing about and factoring into your thinking as it may contribute to the solution. The main thrust of this approach is to help your dog feel safe by showing him how little the sound means to you. Confidence. Try to look anywhere else but at your dog when you hear a noise that might affect him. Stay relaxed and continue what you were doing beforehand, as though you heard nothing. You can use your peripheral vision to take a sneaky peek at what he's doing after a few seconds but avoid making too much direct eye contact at this point. By not reacting you are communicating that the sound holds no significance for you ... the idea being that your dog will grow in confidence and become less reactive to this sound over time.

3) Avoid nurturing the wrong colour

Many people, on hearing a loud bang, see their dog's worried face, timid body language and demeanour and, naturally, feel very upset for him. A common reaction often involves someone in the household, often more than one person, going over to where their dog has taken refuge and petting him in a very concerned and comforting way. This person is also very likely to talk quietly and repeatedly to their dog in order to soothe him, desperate to reassure him that everything will be okay. Many people will stay beside their troubled dog throughout the entire ordeal, stroking and cuddling him lovingly so he can feel supported in a time of confusion. This way of thinking is loving and very well-intentioned but the approach is applying human psychology to a canine behaviour and is not considering the colours of the mind or associations at all. If you've ever tried to soothe an anxious dog in this situation using this 'lavishing affection' approach, even though *you* might feel much better about the situation knowing that you tried to help, the next time he hears 'that noise' it's very likely that your actions will not have reduced the dog's level of reactivity to the stimulus and he will quickly find that troubled state of mind again. Your dog will also recognise instantly that you're talking to him soothingly and differently to any tone of voice you would normally use—he might even interpret this as evidence that you're nervous and amber too ... maybe you're sitting or kneeling down beside him because the noises obviously made you feel uncomfortable and you're seeking refuge too? If you—his teacher—is concerned, then your dog's take on things is that he was right to be worried and the fear cycle rolls on. It's completely appropriate and helpful to offer some comfort and reassurance (see point 5 below: 'Using gentle contact to soothe') by massaging your dog while using some kind words and sharing a confident and warm vibe, but try to avoid nurturing the wrong colour by lavishing only 'concerned affection' all the time. It can be a difficult line to walk but try to focus on sharing a very kind/confident and practical vibe rather than only a very sympathetic and emotional one.

Some people also offer treats to a dog that's in this nervous state/colour, hopeful that he'll be distracted or coaxed out of his anxiety using food. While the human will feel fabulous if their (anxious) trainee takes a few tasty morsels, it's very unlikely to happen ... any animal under a serious amount of stress won't ever entertain food. Please avoid bringing treats or food into the equation here as this will only confuse the issue and your dog.

4) Offer security

Aside from not showing any reaction to 'that noise' and trying to avoid nurturing the wrong colour, you can also help the situation by closing your curtains or blinds and do your best to muffle any external sounds by turning the volume up on the radio or TV … or both.

Another very positive thing to do for a dog that fears these noises might be to recreate a natural dark den, one where he can settle down inside the home and retreat to for the duration of 'that noise'. In this way, you're giving him the best possible chance of being as comfortable as possible during the event. You could place a crate in a quiet area of the home and drape a throw or heavy blanket over it, leaving only the area around the (open) crate door slightly uncovered. Alternatively, put his bed under a table/desk in the corner of a room and make a dark hide for him by draping a blanket over any exposed areas. Get your dog accustomed to this arrangement (by placing treats in there now and again) while there's no loud noise or drama happening so he knows he always has this positive and quiet place to go to (and come out of) whenever he likes.

5) Using gentle contact to soothe

If you have Martha, a very frightened dog living at home, clearly desperate for your attention and affection whenever 'that noise' is heard—determined to velcro herself to you—there is a 'gentle contact' approach that can work well when soothing. Some people offer a calm head massage to a stressed trainee who is sitting on the floor next to them, others simply invite their dog onto the couch alongside them or onto their laps, resting an arm/hand on their trainee for some reassurance. Very little talking takes place but you can say something like, "Settle, Martha" calmly as you massage. If you interact and communicate like this, many dogs will feel very comforted/safe and will benefit from being right next to their confident and green teacher. You might consider putting a thunder shirt on Martha as well (provided she is already used to it and likes wearing it) to help increase the level of gentle contact during a difficult time.

6) <u>Be careful with aversion therapy</u>

Some older schools of thought might have recommended various forms of aversion therapy as potential solutions to noise sensitivity issues like these. Such approaches ask a dog to actively engage in the very activity that's proving upsetting for him—this is called 'flooding'—and through repeated exposure, fear levels can sometimes decrease. One example might involve taking a dog (who is a little fearful of fireworks) out on walks at times when you know fireworks are likely to go off. If your trainee feels threatened or alarmed whenever he hears screaming children, then an aversion strategy might involve setting up a role-play with a few older children to make their 'special screaming noise' when your dog is nearby. It's not only exposing the dog to the noise or event repeatedly that can make a difference, but regularly exposing him to your positive vibe alongside that's consistently saying, "I'm confident, there's nothing to worry about" is another key component here. Over time, the intention is that your trainee will understand that nothing terrible ever happens and he'll get more comfortable with these events.

While these methods can build confidence in some dogs that are only *mildly* worried by certain noises, many professionals believe they would be *most* unsuitable and prove far too traumatic for those dogs that are clearly worried or even terrified in such circumstances. Dogs that get quite anxious should NOT be asked to engage in any aversive sessions, as this kind of strategy is only likely to make them feel petrified and will make matters much worse. Dogs like this should stay indoors when 'that noise' is sounding and be allowed to build up their confidence levels gradually while feeling safe.

7) Play some recordings

Provided your dog is only *mildly* affected by a particular noise, you could try accelerating his journey to feeling a little better about 'that noise' by purchasing a commercial recording of firework sounds or claps of thunder, etc. The internet can provide a great source of information so do a little research and find an app or recording that suits your needs.

Then introduce this tool very gently by playing it *quietly* at random times in the day, only for around five seconds at a time initially. An important point to make here is to start by playing these sounds at a level that your trainee *just detects* and never at a level that will present significant stress. Another very important point is to engage your trainee in some activity before and while you play the recording. If he's in the middle of playing a game of retrieve with a tennis ball in the back garden and is already really involved in the game, this is an appropriate time to start playing the recording *quietly* for a very short period. Behave as though you can't hear anything and continue interacting with your dog and the game as before and, once the five seconds have finished, stop the recording and continue the game a while longer. Do the exercise a few times a week and *gradually* increase the duration of this 'playing time' and the volume, so your trainee gets used to the sounds and realises in time that nothing awful ever happens and 'that noise' always stops quite quickly. Practice at the same level until your trainee is quite comfortable with it and then raise the bar very slightly. This gradual desensitising approach really can help some dogs, but you need to use the 'a little a lot' rule when practising.

A key point too is that 'context' is very relevant to dogs in terms of how they associate and learn. If your trainee is completely fine with a firework recording played in your lounge, don't automatically assume he'll still be relaxed if he hears the sound again when in the garden. From your dog's perspective this can seem like two very different events so he might still be very worried by the sound in a new context. The message here is to play the recordings for very short periods, at a low level and in different places (while engaging him in an activity), so he learns to be more relaxed wherever he is when he hears 'that noise.'

8) DAPs and Thunder shirts

DAPs, as outlined earlier, are *D*og *A*ppeasing *P*heromones and come in a spray, plug-in dispenser and collar form. These can be an effective part of the solution and are worth investigating. Thunder shirts/jackets are body wraps that apply gentle, constant and comforting pressure on key areas of a dog's body. Wearing these shirts can help change your dog's mindset at times of stress. Leading thunder shirt manufacturers claim very favourable success rates in helping with issues like fear of thunder or fireworks, so think about doing some research to explore if this is likely to be helpful for your trainee.

9) Homeopathic remedy

You could explore natural rescue remedies for dogs—some people use these to help their dogs feel more relaxed throughout the day and at sensitive times. Some people swear by Aconite and Valerian, for example, as these homeopathic remedies often help counter anxiety.

10) Professional advice

If you are genuinely concerned about your trainee's overall health and wellbeing given that he gets *very worried* by certain noises at times, consider making an appointment to see an experienced trainer/behaviourist and your vet, so you can get some face-to-face advice and practical support to improve your dog's lot during these very stressful times.

Conclusion

Given that we have been considering your dog's perspective up to this point, it seems only right to continue this theme as we draw to a close. So, if your trainee was asked to jot down a few crucial points his human family might use as a guide, a reminder, so everyone can have a happy and contented life together ... he might compose something like the following:

- Do your research and feed me a balanced nutritious diet. Feed quality.
- Exercise and stimulate me daily, inside and outside the home.
- Let me meet up with some (balanced) doggy friends regularly.
- Figure out how I learn best—through play or by using treats and toys—and communicate effectively with me using clear voice commands and some hand signals. Be a very positive, fair and consistent teacher.
- Think about joining a good training group, so we can have a great time learning and practising together.
- Practice on-lead 'Dog Yoga' with me frequently.
- Have FUN with me. Lots of it.
- Try to stay green or low amber ... even though I might make this very difficult for you at times!

I really hope you enjoyed reading this insight into your dog's perspective and the world of dog training. By tuning into your 'colours and vibe' system alongside having clear strategies in place when teaching man's best friend, your trainee will associate you with kindness, clarity, fun and fulfilment. A great partnership is very likely to blossom in no time at all.

Please tell your friends and colleagues about

LoveK9: ***Colours of the Mind***

and leave a review on social media

so, together, we can help people and dogs

by spreading good practice.

Thank you.

Consider joining our group on Facebook

by visiting

https://www.facebook.com/groups/**lovek9**